COMPELLING CONVERSATIONS – JAPAN

*Questions & Quotations
for High-Intermediate Japanese
English Language Learners*

Eric H. Roth

Shiggy Ichinomiya

and

Brent Warner

Foreword by Richard Jones

CHIMAYO PRESS

Compelling Conversations – Japan:
Questions & Quotations for High-Intermediate
Japanese English Language Learners

Copyright @Eric H. Roth and Chimayo Press

By Eric H. Roth, Shiggy Ichinomiya, and Brent Warner
Edited by Toni Aberson and Laurie Selik
Foreword by Richard Jones

Photographs by Shiggy Ichinomiya, Laurie Selik, Dreamtime, and onedollarphoto.com
Published 9/1/ 2015

Roth, Eric H. (Eric Hermann), 1961- author.
Compelling conversations – Japan :
questions & quotations for high intermediate Japanese-English language learners /
Eric H. Roth, Shiggy Ichinomiya and Brent Warner.
pages cm
Includes index.

LCCN 2014952797
ISBN 978-0-9847985-7-5 (paperback)
ISBN 978-0-9847985-8-2 (e-book)

1. English language – Textbooks for foreign speakers –
Japanese. 2. English language – Conversation and phrase
books – Japanese. 3. Quotations, English.
I. Ichinomiya, Shiggy, author. II. Warner, Brent, author.
III. Title.

PE1130.J3R68 2015   428.3'4956
                           QBI15-600141

Chimayo Press
3766 Redwood Ave.
Los Angeles, CA 90066-3506
www.ChimayoPress.com
www.CompellingConversations.com

Telephone: 01-310-390-0131
1-855-ESL-Book (inside US and Canada)
1-855-375-2665

Dedicated to Marianne Ichinomiya
(1932–2012)

Born in Germany, Marianne moved to the United States in 1967 and married Shigemitsu Ichinomiya the next year. Marianne learned English by simply circling words she didn't know in newspapers, books, or magazines. She would then look words up in a hardback American Heritage dictionary. Through English, Marianne created new possibilities for herself. Her life and decisions taught her that you could achieve almost anything with determination, focus, and hard work. A lover of travel and cultures, Marianne found that English provided a bridge to many new ideas, different opinions, and new friendships across the globe.

~⌒

Dedicated to David Russell Hammer
(1925–2015)

He ran a long, strong race and found strength in literature and love.

~⌒

And to the resilient people of Japan who have created a distinctive, evolving culture.

We build too many walls and not enough bridges.
—Isaac Newton (1643–1727), English physicist, mathematician, and scientist

BECOMING A BETTER CONVERSATIONALIST IN ENGLISH

There is a saying in English that someone is a "good conversationalist." This phrase can have many meanings; the phrase may suggest that someone is quite interesting to talk to, has a number of fascinating stories, or loves to engage in a spirited debate. However, on a basic level, being a good conversationalist means that one listens and responds to a conversational partner and keeps the discussion going in a thoughtful manner.

In this sense, a conversation is like a friendly game of volleyball; one needs to keep the ball in the air and the game in action. In a conversation, keeping the game going requires paying attention to the way the conversation is directed toward you and then passing the conversation thoughtfully back to a partner.

Compelling Conversations – Japan covers a wide variety of topics. This book allows you to practice keeping a conversation flowing in many directions. It touches on current events, such as the upcoming Tokyo 2020 Olympics, as well as traditions and everyday aspects of life in Japan and abroad. Through these discussions, it offers opportunities for speakers to engage with each other in various "settings," thus enabling learners to master the skills needed in conversations outside the classroom.

There are, of course, differences in conversational styles among languages and cultures. A common image of English speakers, and in particular Americans, is that they desire to fill up any silence with talk; that is, they talk a lot! This idea is not always correct, but it is true that English speakers in general are less comfortable with longer silence in conversations. A prolonged pause when speaking with others is often referred to as an "awkward silence," and as a matter of politeness we try to avoid these longer gaps in conversations. That is not to say one must keep speaking all the time; we all have said at one time or another, "that guy just *never* stops talking!" *Compelling Conversations – Japan* builds fluency by allowing learners to practice the art and rhythm of English language conversation.

Japan is home to some of the world's most famous historical landmarks and respected international companies. It also hosts, or has hosted, events ranging from Fuji Rock and the Tokyo International Film Festival to the 2006 World Cup games. These settings are among the many in Japan that provide opportunities of intercultural communication. Have you recently used English in such cultural gatherings? Why?

On a broader level, the authors believe in the truth of Wittgenstein's observation that "The limits of my language are the limits of my world." For most, learning a second language is not easy; I can attest to the difficulties of learning to converse in Japanese. However, speaking another language opens many wonderful doors, on both the personal and professional level. *Compelling Conversations – Japan* will help you open these doors in English, and I wish you the best in exploring what lies beyond them.

Richard Jones lived and worked in Japan for ten years. He has an M.Ed. in TESOL (Teaching English to Speakers of Other Languages) from Temple University, Japan, and an M.A. in East Asian Studies with a concentration on Japanese Literature and Culture from UCLA.

INTRODUCTION

Dear English Student:

Speaking English clearly and creating good conversations in English can open many new doors for you in Japan, across Asia, and around the world.

Do you want to make new international friends? Do you want to talk about movies, restaurants, and memories with native English speakers? Do you want a better job in Japan? Or do you plan to succeed in an American college and need to participate more in class discussions? Have you considered traveling and using English as an international language? Have you wondered about living in Australia, England, or the United States?

This American English conversation textbook for Japanese English language learners will help you become more fluent in English. It will also help you become more confident speaking English and become who you want to be in English.

These activities will help you to:

✦ Ask clear, simple questions in English

✦ Listen to each other in English

✦ Respond to questions in English

✦ Understand other English speakers better

✦ Become more comfortable speaking English

✦ Use common conversation starters in English

✦ Learn how to continue conversations on many topics

✦ Discover and use new English vocabulary words

✦ Memorize some American sayings

✦ Recall some Japanese proverbs in English

✦ Discuss ideas by studying classical and modern quotations in English

✦ Express your opinions and support your statements in English

✦ Find and share Internet resources about modern life in English

✦ Speak English with greater confidence in Japan and abroad

✦ Learn more about your Japanese classmates and yourself in English

You may have heard the phrase, "Practice makes perfect." We prefer the more practical observation, "Practice makes progress." Our goal is for you to make significant, meaningful, and verifiable progress in every chapter.

You will learn by doing and creating real, meaningful conversations in English.

Let's begin!

TABLE OF CONTENTS

CHAPTERS

RESOURCES & NOTES

1

GETTING THE CONVERSATION STARTED

Speaking English allows people to express themselves in an international language. In these lessons, you will work with other students. You will be asking questions about their experiences, and you will be answering questions. In these ways, you will be practicing English, learning about other cultures, and practicing ways to make conversation pleasant and interesting. You will create compelling conversations in English and have fun.

VOCABULARY WARM-UP

Which words do you already know? Underline them, and circle the words you are unsure about. Then review your answers with a partner.

agree	argue	conversation	courage	disagree
discourage	encourage	gesture	proverb	quotation

ACTIVITY 1: SHARING EXPERIENCES

Your teacher will pair you with a partner. In conversation, it is often helpful to show other people that we understand what they wish to communicate. A smile, a nod of the head, and eye contact show that you are interested in what your partner is saying and invite your partner to continue. Frowning, shaking one's head no, or looking away while others are speaking may discourage them from continuing the conversation. Interrupting, too, may prevent the other person from sharing thoughts. Positive feedback often helps others build confidence.

In this class, we want to encourage each other. Take turns answering the following questions about English. Remember, "A journey of a thousand miles must begin with a single step." (Optional: write down your partner's answers in this book after asking each question.)

1. Why do you want to learn English? Give three reasons.

   a.

   b.

   c.

2. How can English help you?

3. What do you think is the fastest way to learn English?

4. How can English improve your life?

5. How do you think you can improve your English?

6. What dream job would you like to have speaking English in Japan? What dream job would you like to have speaking English outside of Japan?

7. Can speaking English give you more options? How?

8. If you had to teach Japanese to a foreigner, what advice would you give them to improve and learn Japanese?

9. How can you take your English ability to a higher level?

10. What will you commit to do to make this happen?

11. How have other Japanese people who have learned English become better speakers?

12. What additional opportunities does fluently speaking English provide?

> ### Culture Corner:
> ### Interrupting in Japanese
>
> Visiting Japan provides many surprises for first-time visitors. The common Japanese conversation trait of using "un" when listening is among these surprises. This use of the "un" sound indicates that the speaker is being carefully listened to.
>
> In the West, however, this type of interjection is often a signal of disinterest. In other words, some Westerners think the Japanese listener is bored. This cultural difference can sometimes cause confusion.
>
> To show you are carefully listening, you might want to nod your head and maintain eye contact when speaking with Western visitors. You can also remain quiet until the speaker has finished the thought.

ACTIVITY 2: EXPANDING VOCABULARY

Look at the definitions and example sentences that follow. Do the definitions match what you and your partner expected in the vocabulary warm-up list? If not, what is different?

---

agree, *verb*: to think the same way as someone else.

✦ *I agree with you.*

argue, *verb*: to give reasons and strongly disagree.

✦ *Is it true that Japanese people do not like to argue?*

conversation, *noun*: talking; exchanging words between two or more people.

✦ *Midori started a conversation with her new English classmate.*

---

courage, *noun*: bravery; the act of facing danger.

✦ *Fumiko showed her <u>courage</u> when she traveled by herself in Southeast Asia.*

disagree, *verb*: to think in a different way; to not agree.

✦ *We <u>disagree</u> about the best place to eat ramen.*

discourage, *verb*: to advise someone against doing something.

✦ *My father <u>discouraged</u> me from smoking. He said smoking is bad for my heart, lungs, and general health.*

encourage, *verb*: to make someone feel good about an action; to say, "Yes you can."

✦ *The Japanese women's soccer coach, Norio Sasaki, <u>encourages</u> the soccer team players to always do their best.*

gesture, *noun*: A movement of the body, especially a hand or the head, to express an idea or meaning.

✦ *The interviewer made a <u>gesture</u> that indicated for me to sit down.*

proverb, *noun*: stating a general truth or piece of advice.

✦ *Yuuji's favorite Japanese <u>proverb</u> is, "Even monkeys fall from trees."*

quotation, *noun*: A group of words taken from a text or speech and repeated by someone other than the original author or speaker.

✦ *<u>Quotations</u> are a great way to share ideas from famous people.*

ACTIVITY 3: ASK MORE QUESTIONS

A. Select five words from the vocabulary list above and write a question for each word. Remember to start your question with a question word (Who, What, Where, When, Why, How, Is, Are, Do, Did, Does, etc.). You will also want to end each question with a question mark (?). Underline each vocabulary word.

✎ Example: How can you <u>encourage</u> a friend to try something new?

1. ....

2. ....

3. ....

4. ....

5. ....

B. Take turns asking and answering questions with your partner.

ACTIVITY 4: PHOTOGRAPHS TO START CONVERSATIONS

Photographs capture moments, inform viewers, and start conversations. In small groups, examine the photograph and discuss the questions that follow.

1. Can you describe this picture?

2. What colors appear in the Australian, American, British, and French flags?

3. What colors often appear in African flags?

4. What are some symbols that appear on flags you know? What do the symbols represent?

5. What is your favorite flag? Why?

6. What is the purpose of a flag?

ACTIVITY 5: PARAPHRASING PROVERBS

Proverbs, or traditional sayings, can show big ideas in a few words. We will use proverbs and famous quotations so we can look at the ideas of many people and cultures and discuss these ideas. We will also often paraphrase, or put into other words, proverbs and discuss quotations to expand our vocabulary.

Paraphrasing is an important skill in both writing and speaking. In this exercise, take turns reading the quotations and proverbs out loud. What does each sentence mean? As a group, paraphrase the proverb by using different words to show the same idea. Remember to encourage each other with words and gestures.

1. You can know ten things by learning one. —Japanese

Meaning: ....

....

2. You catch more flies with honey than with vinegar. —Greek

Meaning: ....

....

3. I hear and I forget. I see and I remember. I do and I understand. —Chinese

Meaning: ....

....

4. We learn by doing. —English

Meaning: ....

....

5. One kind word can warm three winter months. —Japanese

Meaning: ....

....

B. Can you add another proverb offering advice?

1. ....

ACTIVITY 6: PRONUNCIATION PRACTICE

You can speak English with a distinctly Japanese accent and still be clearly understood. However, reducing confusing sounds can greatly improve your communication with English speakers and help to eliminate confusion in your English conversations.

In each chapter we will focus on one pronunciation issue. Pay careful attention to that issue as you continue to talk with your classmates and English teacher.

"L" and "r" are perhaps the most frequently confused sounds for Japanese learners of English. This pronunciation pattern is because there is only one "in-between" sound in Japanese, which is often written in roman letters as "ra-ri-ru-re-ro." For native English speakers, though, "l" and "r" are two distinct sounds. The "l" sound is made by pressing your tongue against the hard spot just above your top teeth. The "r" sound is made by pulling the tip of your tongue back and not touching anything in your mouth.

THUMBS UP / THUMBS DOWN GAME

Choose a partner to work with for the following activity. Partner A will choose *any* word on the "l" words list below and say it out loud. If partner A says an "l" word, partner B gives the thumbs up sign. If they say an "r" word, partner B should give the thumbs down sign. When you get three thumbs up in a row, switch roles.

"l" words	"r" words
lice	rice
light	right
long	wrong
play	pray
lock	rock
clown	crown
pilot	pirate
belly	berry
clash	crash
splint	sprint

ACTIVITY 7: THE CONVERSATION CONTINUES

Let's continue to explore the importance of communication in our lives with one or two classmates. Use complete sentences to respond.

1. Who is your favorite person to have long conversations with? Why?

2. Do you sometimes disagree with your friends? What do you disagree about?

3. Have you ever been impressed by someone with whom you disagree? Why?

4. Do you regularly meet or speak with foreigners? In your experience, how do they communicate differently from Japanese people?

5. Some people say they don't feel comfortable speaking with foreigners. How would you encourage them to try?

6. Can you remember your last argument? With whom did you argue? Why?

7. When you want to learn something new, how do you find the motivation?

8. Is it easier to study when you are younger or older? Why do you think so?

9. Who was your favorite teacher? Why did you like him or her?

10. What is your favorite Japanese proverb? Can you translate it into English? What does it mean?

11. Some people believe that only a small percentage of communication is through words. Do you agree? Why or why not?

12. Are you good at getting people to agree with you? If so, how do you do it? If not, what do you think is missing?

13. Have you ever felt misunderstood? What can we do to be better understood?

14. When do you feel the most motivated? What motivates you to do your best?

ACTIVITY 8: DISCUSSING QUOTATIONS

Do you agree or disagree?

Take turns reading these quotations out loud and discuss them with your partner. Do you agree with the quotation? Disagree? Why? Afterwards, pick a favorite quotation by circling the number and explain your choice. Remember to give a reason or example.

1. "Conversation means being able to disagree and still continue the discussion."
   —*Dwight MacDonald (1906–1982), American editor*

   ☐ Agree   ☐ Disagree

   Why? ....

2. "Be curious, not judgmental."
   —*Walt Whitman (1819–1892), American poet*

   ☐ Agree   ☐ Disagree

   Why? ....

3. "There is always hope when people are forced to listen to both sides."
   —*John Steward Mill (1806–1873), British philosopher*

   ☐ Agree   ☐ Disagree

   Why? ....

4. "You can make more friends in two months by becoming interested in other people than you can in two years by trying to get other people interested in you."
   —*Dale Carnegie (1888–1955), American writer, lecturer*

   ☐ Agree   ☐ Disagree

   Why? ....

5. "Do what you can, with what you have, where you are."
   —*Theodore Roosevelt (1858–1919), 26th U.S. President*

   ☐ Agree   ☐ Disagree

   Why? ....

6. "It is difficult to understand the universe if you only study one planet."
   —*Musashi Miyamoto (1584–1685), Japanese warrior and author of* The Book of Five Rings

   ☐ Agree   ☐ Disagree

   Why? ....

7. "The less you talk, the more you are listened to."
   —*Abigail Van Buren (1918–2013), American advice columnist*

   ☐ Agree   ☐ Disagree

   Why? ....

8. "When a woman is talking to you, listen to what she says with her eyes."
   —*Victor Hugo (1802–1885), French poet, playwright, novelist, essayist*

   ☐ Agree   ☐ Disagree

   Why? ....

9. "I never learn anything talking. I only learn things when I ask questions."
   —*Lou Holtz (1937–), retired American football coach*

   ☐ Agree   ☐ Disagree

   Why? ....

10. "Don't be afraid to make a mistake. But make sure you don't make the same mistake twice."
    —*Akio Morita (1921–1999), Japanese chairman of Sony Corporation*

    ☐ Agree   ☐ Disagree

    Why? ....

My favorite quote was: ....

....

Why? ....

ACTIVITY 9: TELL ME ABOUT JAPAN ... IN ENGLISH

People want to know about Japan and Japanese culture. Next time you travel abroad or meet a foreigner, you can tell them about Japan in English.

A Conversation Is Like a River

A skilled conversationalist may guide the conversation, but it also may choose to go in its own direction. Rather than resisting the conversation, go with the flow and enjoy the unexpected pleasures that may pop up or emerge.

With your partner, think of three questions about the *Daruma* doll and provide the answers.

1Q. ....

A. ....

2Q. ....

A. ....

3Q. ....

A. ....

What else do you know about the *Daruma* doll that might be interesting to foreigners in Japan?

1. ....

2. ....

3. ....

SEARCH and SHARE

Reviewing Pronunciation Tips on the Internet

Student Name: .... Date: ....

Class: .... Teacher: ....

Find a YouTube video clip that gives tips or suggestions on improving English pronunciation. Look for ways to clearly make sounds to be better understood in English. You can also search for common word stress patterns in English. Watch the video, listen carefully, take notes, and share the pronunciation tips with your classmates.

Video title: ....

Web address: ....

Length: .... Creator: ....

1. Describe the video.

2. What pronunciation tips did the video give?

3. Which words or sounds did the video focus on?

4. How practical did you find the advice? Why?

5. What was the strongest part? Why?

6. What was the weakest part? Why?

7. Who do you think is the target audience for this video? Why?

8. Why did you choose this video?

9. How would you rate this video on a scale of 1–5, with 5 being the highest? Why?

> **"I was the kind nobody thought could make it. I had a funny Boston accent. I couldn't pronounce my R's. I wasn't a beauty."**
>
> —*Barbara Walters (1929–), American television journalist*

2

GOING BEYOND HELLO

VOCABULARY WARM-UP

Which words do you already know? Underline them, and circle the words you are unsure about. Then review your answers with a partner.

appreciate	enthusiasm	frown	goal	impression
interview	possession	recommend	sibling	suburb

ACTIVITY 1: TELLING YOUR STORY

Interview the person sitting next to you. Take turns talking, write notes, and prepare to introduce your partner to our class. Feel free to add or omit any questions that you wish. Challenge yourself by speaking full sentences instead of short, one-word answers. Let's begin!

1. What is your last name? First name?

2. Do you have a nickname? If yes, what is it?

3. Who chose your name? Why? Do you like your first name?

4. What is your favorite Western name for a girl? A guy?

5. Do you have any older brothers? Sisters? Younger siblings?

6. Where did you grow up in Japan? Is that a city, a village, or a suburb?

7. What were you like as a child? Playful? Happy? Curious? Shy? Have you changed?

8. What topics do you like to talk about when meeting someone for the first time?

9. What are a few things you do not talk about when you meet someone for the first time?

10. Do you have a favorite possession from your childhood? Why is it important to you?

11. Are you left-handed? Right-handed? What happens when you try to write with your other hand?

12. What is your favorite color? Number? Season? Why?

13. What kind of music do you listen to? Rock 'n' roll? Jazz? Classical? Hip-hop? J-Pop?

14. Do you have a favorite musician or rock group? Which songs do you like?

15. Which is your favorite radio station or television channel? Why?

Culture Corner:
Blood Type

Many Japanese citizens believe that blood type relates to your personality. In turn, many Japanese are surprised to find that Westerners rarely believe in the connection between blood type and personality. In fact, many Westerners do not even know their own blood type for medical reasons, and this ignorance can cause serious problems during accidents. Do you know your blood type? What is it? Why is your blood type important?

ACTIVITY 2: EXPANDING YOUR VOCABULARY

Look at the definitions and example sentences that follow. Do the definitions match what you and your partner expected in the vocabulary warm-up list? If not, what is different?

appreciate, *verb*: to feel thankful for something; to like and see the value in something.

+ *Hiromi appreciates her friends and family.*

enthusiasm, *noun*: excitement; a passion for someone or something.

+ *Shigeo showed his enthusiasm by loudly cheering for the Yomiuri Giants.*

frown, *noun*: a face of sadness or disapproval where the mouth curves downward at both ends.

+ *Junko is usually happy; however, this morning she had a frown on her face.*

frown, *verb*: to show unhappiness or displeasure with the face; the opposite of smile.

+ *She frowned in the mirror but smiled when she saw her best friend.*

goal, *noun*: a target; a desired result.

+ *My goal is to travel to one new country each year.*

impression, *noun*: a mental "picture" left by a person, place, or thing in another's mind.

   ✦ *A good first <u>impression</u> is important when looking for a job.*

interview, *noun*: a formal conversation.

   ✦ *My job <u>interview</u> lasted 20 minutes, and the manager wants to interview me again next week.*

interview, *verb*: to ask someone questions to gain more information.

   ✦ *The company president <u>interviewed</u> over 20 people before she hired the best candidate.*

possession, *noun*: an object that one holds or owns.

   ✦ *Naoko's favorite <u>possession</u> is a kimono that her grandmother gave her years ago.*

recommend, *verb*: to advise; to give your opinion.

   ✦ *I <u>recommend</u> you try real Kobe beef if you ever visit Kansai.*

sibling, *noun*: brother or sister in the same family.

   ✦ *Sakura has two <u>siblings</u>: a younger brother and an older sister.*

suburb, *noun*: an area where people live outside a city.

   ✦ *I work in Osaka, but I live in Rokko-michi, a small <u>suburb</u> where it's quieter and cheaper.*

ACTIVITY 3: ASK MORE QUESTIONS

A. Select five words from the vocabulary list and write a question for each word. Remember to start your question with a question word (Who, What, Where, When, Why, How, Is, Are, Do, Did, Does, etc.). You will also want to end each question with a question mark (?). Underline each vocabulary word.

✎ Example: What restaurants do you <u>recommend</u>?

1. ....

2. ....

3. ....

4. ....

5. ....

B. Take turns asking and answering questions with your partner or group members.

ACTIVITY 4: PHOTOGRAPHS TO START CONVERSATIONS

Photographs capture moments, inform viewers, and start conversations. In small groups, examine the photograph and discuss the questions that follow.

1. Can you describe these pictures?

2. When do you shake hands and when do you bow?

3. Have you ever had an awkward handshake? What made it awkward?

4. What makes a good handshake? How would you describe it?

5. What are the rules of bowing? When should you bow more deeply?

6. How many times do you bow on an average day?

ACTIVITY 5: PARAPHRASING PROVERBS

A. Read the proverbs below. Write what you think they mean in the spaces provided.

1. Flattery is the best persuader of people. —Japanese

Meaning: ....

....

2. Strangers are just friends you haven't met yet. —American

Meaning: ....

....

3. A single conversation across the table with a wise person is worth a month's study of books. —Chinese

Meaning: ....

....

4. You never get a second chance to make a first impression. —American

Meaning: ....

....

5. Obey the customs of the village you enter. —Japanese

Meaning: ....

....

B. Can you add another proverb about meeting people?

1.   ....

ACTIVITY 6: PRONUNCIATION PRACTICE

You can speak English with a distinctly Japanese accent and still be clearly understood. However, reducing confusing sounds can greatly improve your communication with English speakers and help to eliminate confusion in your English conversations.

"B" AND "V"

Without a natural "v" sound in Japanese, many Japanese people often replace it with a "b" sound. This pronunciation creates confusion for many native English speakers. English has several words with similar sounds.

On the other hand, the "b" sound is common in Japanese, and shouldn't create any problems. It is the same as "ba-bi-bu-be-bo."

The "v" sound should be formed the same way as making an "f" sound. Put your upper teeth on your lower lip, and push air out gently. Then, add your voice to the sound. This mouth movement should make the "v" sound.

MINIMAL PAIR BINGO

As a class or in pairs, choose one person to call out random words from the board. When a student has gotten five consecutive choices, say "bingo." Check against the real answers to make sure the student did not mishear any of the words spoken. The winner gets to call out the next set of words, and the bingo game can continue.

	B	I	N	G	O
1	berry	vet	beer	vote	vase
2	vent	van	best	veer	rebel
3	bale	bat	⭐	very	veil
4	boat	dub	base	bent	ban
5	vat	bet	vest	revel	dove

ACTIVITY 7: THE CONVERSATION CONTINUES

Let's continue to explore going beyond hello with one or two classmates. Use complete sentences to respond.

1. What do you like to do outside? Why?

2. Where do you go to walk or hike?

3. What is your favorite sport? Why?

4. How do you like to spend your free time? What interests you?

5. Do you have a hobby? Do you collect anything? How long have you enjoyed it?

6. What makes you smile? Where do you feel most comfortable?

7. What are some things that might cause you to frown?

8. Have you ever been interviewed before? If so, why?

9. Do you have a favorite English or Japanese word or expression? Why?

10. What are your goals for this year? Why? What is your plan?

11. How would your friends describe you? What would you add?

12. What are three things that you appreciate about living in Japan?

ACTIVITY 8: DISCUSSING QUOTATIONS

Take turns reading these quotations out loud and discuss them with your partner. Do you agree with the quotation? Disagree? Why? Afterwards, pick a favorite quotation by circling the number and explain your choice. Remember to give a reason or example.

1. "There is nothing in the whole world so painful as feeling that one is not liked."
   —*Sei Shōnagon (966–1017?), Japanese author of* The Pillow Book
   ☐ Agree   ☐ Disagree
   Why? ....

2. "I never met a man I didn't like."
   —*Will Rogers (1879–1935), American humorist*
   ☐ Agree   ☐ Disagree
   Why? ....

3. "I have always depended on the kindness of strangers."
   —*Tennessee Williams (1911–1983), American writer, playwright*
   ☐ Agree   ☐ Disagree
   Why? ....

4. "They (my parents) would give me an African name, Barack, or blessed, believing that in a tolerant America, your name is no barrier to success."
   —*Barack H. Obama (1961–), 44th U.S. President*
   ☐ Agree   ☐ Disagree
   Why? ....

5. "Never let your fear of striking out get in your way."
   —*Babe Ruth (1895–1948), American baseball legend*

   ☐ Agree   ☐ Disagree

   Why? ....

6. "There's a difference between solitude and loneliness. I can understand the concept of being a monk for a while."
   —*Tom Hanks (1956–), American actor, director, producer*

   ☐ Agree   ☐ Disagree

   Why? ....

7. "Everything becomes a little different as soon as it is spoken out loud."
   —*Hermann Hesse (1877–1962), German novelist and 1946 Nobel Prize winner*

   ☐ Agree   ☐ Disagree

   Why? ....

8. "I am simple, complex, generous, selfish, unattractive, beautiful, lazy and driven."
   —*Barbra Streisand (1942–), American singer, actress, director, producer*

   ☐ Agree   ☐ Disagree

   Why? ....

9. "We keep moving forward, opening new doors, and doing new things, because we're curious and curiosity keeps leading us down new paths."
   —*Walt Disney (1901–1966), American cartoonist and entrepreneur*

   ☐ Agree   ☐ Disagree

   Why? ....

10. "Successful people ask better questions, and as a result, they get better answers."
    —*Tony Robbins (1960–), American self-help author*

    ☐ Agree   ☐ Disagree

    Why? ....

My favorite quote was: ....

....

Why? ....

ACTIVITY 9: TELL ME ABOUT JAPAN ... IN ENGLISH

People want to know about Japan and Japanese culture. Next time you travel abroad or meet foreigners, you can tell them about Japan in English.

CHOPSTICK ETIQUETTE

Many foreigners are not used to eating with chopsticks. Can you think of some rules or hints to share when using chopsticks? Here is an example:

Do not leave chopsticks sticking up vertically in rice. This is only done at funerals with rice that is put onto the altar.

Think of three more things that visitors to Japan might need to know about chopsticks. How can you explain the rules?

1. ....

2. ....

3. ....

With your partner, can you ask and answer three questions about chopsticks?

For example: When are chopsticks better than forks?

1Q. ....

A. ....

2Q. ....

A. ....

3Q. ....

A. ....

SEARCH and SHARE

Interviewing English Speakers and Tourists

Student Name: .... Date: ....

Class: .... Teacher: ....

Go to a local tourist site, find someone on campus, or meet a neighbor in your neighborhood. Choose a few questions to interview English speakers. Many native English speakers will be happy to help you practice your English conversation skills and share their experiences for a few minutes.

1. Can I ask you a few short questions for my English class?

2. Where are you from?

3. Why did you come to ....?

4. How much time have you spent in .... so far?

5. What do you like most about being in ....?

6. What have you seen so far in ....?

7. What traditional dishes have you eaten so far?

8. Have you found any bargains shopping yet? What?

9. How do you travel from one place to another? Do you walk? Take a bus? Other?

10. What are you planning on doing tomorrow?

11. Will you be going to ....?

12. Do you expect to go to ....?

13. What are some other places you would like to see in ....? Why?

14. How would you describe your time in .... so far? Why?

15. Would you recommend visiting .... to your family and friends?

Remember to thank your conversation partner for their time and wish them a good day.

> **"Tourists don't know where they've been;**
> **travelers don't know where they're going."**
> —*Paul Theroux (1941–), American writer and novelist*

3

HOME SWEET HOME

VOCABULARY WARM-UP

Which words do you already know? Underline them, and circle the words you are unsure about. Then review your answers with a partner.

appliance	checklist	exterior	fee	homesick
interior	lease	neighbor	neighborhood	residence

ACTIVITY 1: SHARING EXPERIENCES

Everybody lives somewhere. Share the story of your home with a conversation partner by responding to these questions. Feel free to add other questions.

1. Can you tell me a bit about your home?

2. How long have you lived there? Your whole life?

3. Do you have any traditional Japanese sliding paper doors (*shoji*) in your house?

4. Do you sleep on a futon or a bed? Which do you prefer?

5. Do you always take your shoes off when entering your home? Why?

6. Why do you think many people in other countries keep their shoes on indoors?

7. What are some ways that people relax at home?

8. Describe what you see from your bedroom window.

9. Which is your favorite room? Why? What does it look like?

10. What are some of the advantages of living in small apartments? The disadvantages?

11. Does your bedroom have *tatami* mats, carpet, tile, or wood flooring? What kind of flooring do you prefer?

12. What paintings, posters, or other artwork do you have in your bedroom?

13. Do you have any pets? What is their favorite spot?

14. What, if any, plants or flowers do you have? Where are they located in your home?

15. How did you find your current home? What were you looking for? Did you have a checklist?

ACTIVITY 2: EXPANDING VOCABULARY

Look at the definitions and example sentences that follow. Do the definitions match what you and your partner expected in the vocabulary warm-up list? If not, what is different?

---

appliance, *noun*: a machine or device that performs particular functions in the office or home; an object with a special use or purpose.

+ *Yumi has a coffee maker and a toaster, but she still wants a microwave and other* <u>*appliances*</u> *for her home.*

checklist, *noun*: a written series of items arranged top to bottom, created to ensure accuracy or completeness.

+ *Hiromi always keeps a shopping* <u>*checklist*</u> *in her purse.*

exterior, *adjective*: the outside; opposite of interior.

+ <u>*Exterior*</u> *paint must be stronger than interior paint because it must protect against the rain.*

---

fee, *noun*: money paid for a service; the cost to use something of value owned by someone else.

> ✦ *You have to pay a <u>fee</u> to register a motorcycle in Matsuyama City.*

homesick, *adjective*: missing one's family or home.

> ✦ *Kaoruko got <u>homesick</u> for her family after two weeks away.*

interior, *noun*: the inside of a house, room, object, or area; the inner part of a place or thing.

> ✦ *The bright <u>interior</u> colors gave the new California fusion restaurant a hip, modern look.*

lease, *noun*: a contract made to obtain the use of something (car, home) for a specified price over a specified period of time; a period of time covered by a lease.

> ✦ *Aya's apartment <u>lease</u> ends next month.*

lease, *verb*: to rent for a specific time period.

> ✦ *Kenji <u>leased</u> a new car after he was hired because his new job required him to drive for work.*

neighbor, *noun*: a person living next door or nearby.

> ✦ *Ayumi's <u>neighbor</u> feeds the cats when she leaves town.*

neighborhood, *noun*: a particular section of a city.

> ✦ *The Kato family likes their <u>neighborhood</u> because it has a lovely park and a good school.*

residence, *noun*: a place one lives; the act or fact of living in a specific place as one's home.

> ✦ *My <u>residence</u> during the school year is in Nagoya, but my true home is in Saitama with my family.*

ACTIVITY 3: ASK MORE QUESTIONS

A. Select five words from the vocabulary list and write a question for each word. Remember to start your question with a question word (Who, What, Where, When, Why, How, Is, Are, Do, Did, Does, etc.). You will also want to end each question with a question mark (?). Underline each vocabulary word.

✎ Example: What is your favorite kitchen <u>appliance</u>? Why?

1. ....

2. ....

3. ....

4. ....

5. ....

B. Take turns asking and answering questions with your partner or group members. Ask your teacher to give you feedback on your questions to check your English grammar.

ACTIVITY 4: PHOTOGRAPHS TO START CONVERSATIONS

Photographs capture moments, inform viewers, and start conversations. In small groups, examine the photograph and discuss the questions that follow.

1. Can you describe this picture?

2. Can koi fish be pets? Do you have any pets? What kind?

3. Have you ever had an aquarium or fish tank? If yes, what kind of fish? If no, why not?

4. Can you think of some famous fish or fictional fish characters?

5. Can you compare fish to dogs or cats as pets? Which would you prefer? Why?

ACTIVITY 5: PARAPHRASING PROVERBS

A. What do these proverbs and sayings mean? Discuss them with your partner. Circle your favorites.

1. Birds return to old nests. —Japanese

Meaning: ....

....

2. Home is where the heart is. —English

Meaning: ....

....

3. Home is where we grumble the most and are treated the best. —American

Meaning: ....

....

4. A house is not a home. —English

Meaning: ....

....

5. A good cup of tea and a bowl of rice at home is better than a banquet somewhere else. —Japanese

Meaning: ....

....

B. Can you add another proverb about homes?

1. ....

Culture Corner:
Home vs. House

What's the difference between a house and a home? English speakers clearly distinguish the two words. A house is simply the building where people live. It's a physical structure. A house can be a stand-alone house, an apartment, or a condo.

A home, however, is the place where people live, create their lives, and feel comfortable. Often, teenagers who are forced to move may feel that their new location is a house, but not a home. They may have no memories there or friends nearby.

Does the expression "A house is not a home" in Activity 5 seem different when you understand this point?

ACTIVITY 6: PRONUNCIATION PRACTICE

You can speak English with a distinctly Japanese accent and still be clearly understood. However, reducing confusing sounds can greatly improve your communication with English speakers and help to eliminate confusion in your English conversations.

"TH" AND "S"

Many Japanese students find the so-called unvoiced "th" sound in English hard to remember. The sound is actually not difficult to make, but it is easy to forget if you don't pay attention. Likewise, the common "s" sound in English is hard to remember. The sound is not difficult to make, but it is easy to forget! This sound is the same as the Japanese "sa-su-se-so," but it is different from "shi".

The unvoiced "th" sound needs to be pronounced by putting your tongue between your teeth (or sticking it out!). Some Japanese students find this embarrassing, but remember, this is English. It's okay to look a little silly!

SILENT SPEAKING

Look at the list of words below. Practice silently "saying" the words without using your voice and making a sound. Your partner should be able to look at your mouth and guess if you are trying to use the "s" sound or the "th" sound.

"s" words	"th" words
mouse	mouth
sing	thing
some	thumb
worse	worth
pass	path
sin	thin
moss	moth
sank	thank
force	fourth
sink	think

How many of the ten silent words did your partner correctly guess? You can repeat the activity and switch roles for more pronunciation practice.

ACTIVITY 7: THE CONVERSATION CONTINUES

Let's continue to explore what home means with one or two classmates. Use complete sentences to respond.

1. When you were a child, did you live in a house or an apartment?

2. What did you like about it? What did you dislike?

3. Which was your favorite room? Why?

4. What is your favorite childhood memory at home?

5. Have you ever felt homesick? What did you miss the most?

6. Is your neighborhood the same today as it was when you were a child? In what ways is it different? In what ways is it the same?

7. What makes a good neighborhood?

8. Would you rather live in an apartment or a house? Why?

9. Would you rather live in a city, a suburb, a small town, or the countryside? Why?

10. Can you suggest some places to find interior design ideas? Where is a good place to buy furniture? Why?

11. What would your dream residence be like? Can you describe it in detail?

12. What modern appliances would your dream house have? Do you have—or want to have—a robot? Why?

13. What are some advantages of an apartment compared to a house?

14. What makes a house a home for you?

Culture Corner:
Can, Might, Should, and Must

What is the difference between the words "can," "might," "should," and "must"?

+ We use "can" to talk about both ability and possibility.
+ We use "might" to discuss the possibility of something.
+ We use "should" to give advice and say something is a good idea.
+ We use "must" to say something has to be done.

Finish the sentences below in a way that reflects your opinion. Be prepared to explain your opinion in a small group discussion.

What is a good neighbor?

A good neighbor can ....

A good neighbor might ....

A good neighbor should ....

A good neighbor must ....

What is a good roommate?

A good roommate can ....

A good roommate might ....

A good roommate should ....

A good roommate must ....

ACTIVITY 8: DISCUSSING QUOTATIONS

Take turns reading these quotations out loud and discuss them with your partner. Do you agree with the quotation? Disagree? Why? Afterwards, pick a favorite quotation by circling the number and explain your choice. Remember to give a reason or example.

1. "He is happiest, be he king or peasant, who finds peace in his home."
   —*Johann Wolfgang von Goethe (1749–1832), German playwright*
   ☐ Agree   ☐ Disagree
   Why? ....

2. "A man's home is his castle."
   —*Sir Edward Coke (1552–1634), English lord/statesman*
   ☐ Agree   ☐ Disagree
   Why? ....

3. "The ache for home lives in all of us. The safe place where we can go as we are and not be questioned."
   —*Maya Angelou (1928–2014), American author and poet*
   ☐ Agree   ☐ Disagree
   Why? ....

4. "A house is not a home unless it contains food and fire for the mind as well as the body."
   —*Benjamin Franklin (1706–1790), American writer, statesman, and scientist*
   ☐ Agree   ☐ Disagree
   Why? ....

5. "Every day is a journey, and the journey itself is home."
   —*Matsuo Basho (1644–1694), Japanese poet*
   ☐ Agree   ☐ Disagree
   Why? ....

6. "No matter under what circumstances you leave it, home does not cease to be home. No matter how you lived there—well or poorly."
   —*Joseph Brodsky (1940–1996), Russian-American poet and 1987 Nobel Prize winner*
   ☐ Agree   ☐ Disagree
   Why? ....

7. "Have nothing in your house that you do not know to be useful, or believe to be beautiful."
—*William Morris (1834–1896), English artist and writer*

☐ Agree   ☐ Disagree

Why? ....

8. "The best way to keep children at home is to make the home atmosphere pleasant, and let the air out of the tires."
—*Dorothy Parker (1893–1967), American writer*

☐ Agree   ☐ Disagree

Why? ....

9. "Better to do a good deed near home than go far away to burn incense."
—*Amelia Earhart (1897–1937), American pilot and aviation pioneer*

☐ Agree   ☐ Disagree

Why? ....

10. "Architecture is basically a container of something. I hope people will enjoy not so much the teacup as the tea."
—*Yoshio Taniguchi (1937–), Japanese architect*

☐ Agree   ☐ Disagree

Why? ....

My favorite quote was: ....

....

Why? ....

Ask Clarifying Questions

Another technique to improve the quality of conversations is to memorize and use key phrases that help the speaker clarify their ideas and explain their reasons. The phrases below can help you improve the quality of your everyday conversations in and out of the English classroom.

CHECKING WHAT SOMEONE MEANS

Sorry, can you repeat that?

Sorry, what do you mean?

Sorry, I don't understand.

What do you mean by that?

Do you mean ...?

In other words ...?

So are you saying ...?

Can you clarify that statement?

Correct me if I'm wrong, but do you mean ...?

Sorry, I'm not sure if I got that. Are you saying ...?

ASKING SOMEONE TO EXPLAIN WHAT THEY MEAN

Why?

Sorry, what does that mean?

Sorry, can you explain what you mean?

Could you tell me more?

Could you expand on that?

What are the implications?

Can you elaborate a bit?

ASKING FOR MORE DETAILS OR REASONS BECAUSE YOU STILL FEEL CONFUSED

Sorry, what exactly do you mean by that?

Sorry, could you go over that again?

Can you share some details so I can better understand?

ACTIVITY 9: TELL ME ABOUT JAPAN ... IN ENGLISH

People want to know about Japan and Japanese culture. Next time you travel abroad or meet a foreigner, you can tell them about Japan in English.

Tatami mats are a new experience for many foreigners in Japan. What do you know about *tatami* mats?

For example: Many "Western-style" homes in Japan still have a *tatami* room. Why is a *tatami* room included? What is the benefit of *tatami*?

How are *tatami* mats made? What qualities should a consumer look for in a good *tatami* mat? Think of three more things visitors to Japan might want to know about *tatami* mats. How can you explain these ideas?

1. ....
2. ....
3. ....

With your partner, can you ask and answer three questions about *tatami* mats?

For example: How much does one *tatami* mat cost?

1Q. ....
A. ....

2Q. ....
A. ....

3Q. ....
A. ....

SEARCH and SHARE

My Dream Home Worksheet

Student Name: .... Date: ....

Class: .... Teacher: ....

Have you ever thought about living in a dream home? Use your imagination, knowledge, and research to describe the dream home where you would like to live. Use the vocabulary learned in this lesson. Imagine the possibilities. Dream big!

1. Location:

2. Who will live in your dream home?

3. What does the outside look like?

4. How many rooms are there?

5. Describe your bedroom.

6. Describe the room where your family gathers.

7. Describe another room.

8. How would you describe the furniture in your dream home?

9. What else makes this home special?

10. What other information or details can you share?

Be prepared to share your dream with your classmates in class. Show your knowledge and research to describe your dream home.

> **"There is a role and function for beauty in our time."**
> —*Tadao Ando (1941–), Japanese architect*

4

EATING AND DRINKING

VOCABULARY WARM-UP

Which words do you already know? Underline them, and circle the words you are unsure about. Then review your answers with a partner.

chef	culinary	decaffeinated	edible	famine
fast	feast	gluttony	savor	vegetarian

ACTIVITY 1: SHARING EXPERIENCES

Everybody eats. Food is both a necessity and a pleasure. It is also a safe and interesting way to learn more about people. Discuss your eating and drinking experiences with a partner.

1. Do you consider eating an activity that you look forward to, or just a necessity? When do you think it is a pleasure? When is it a chore?

2. What did you eat yesterday for breakfast, lunch, and dinner? Was it a typical day?

3. Do you drink juice, tea, or coffee in the morning? Do you prefer regular or decaf* tea or coffee?

4. Do you eat at the same time every day? Or do you eat when it fits your schedule?

5. Do you prefer salty snacks or sweet snacks? Do you have a sweet tooth?

6. How much do you care about what you eat?

7. What drinks do you enjoy with your evening meal?

8. Which kind of food do you like: Beef? Pork? Poultry? Or do you not like meat?

9. What is your favorite vegetable? Are you a vegetarian? Vegan? Do you know any vegetarians?

10. What is your favorite fruit? Which fruits do you find delicious?

11. Can you name two non-Japanese dishes that you really savor?

12. Which Japanese dishes would you recommend to a tourist? Why?

13. Can you think of some junk food? When do you eat junk food?

14. Do you think Japanese food is healthier than Western food? Why or why not?

15. Do you ever buy food from a convenience store? Why or why not?

*Most people say "decaf" as an abbreviated version of decaffeinated.

ACTIVITY 2: EXPANDING VOCABULARY

Look at the definitions and example sentences that follow. Do the definitions match what you and your partner expected in the vocabulary warm-up list? If not, what is different?

---

chef, *noun*: a professional cook; the head cook in a restaurant.

 ✦ *Our chef is a professional who prepares and cooks delicious meals on a budget.*

culinary, *adjective*: having to do with cooking and food; concerning superior preparation of food.

 ✦ *Study the culinary arts if you want to become a chef.*

decaffeinated, *adjective*: containing no caffeine; a drink with the caffeine removed.

 ✦ *Sue drank decaffeinated coffee because regular coffee made her hyperactive.*

---

edible, *adjective*: something that can be eaten.

  ✦ *Some people find all parts of a fish to be <u>edible</u>.*

famine, *noun*: a great shortage of food where people cannot find enough to eat.

  ✦ *The terrible <u>famine</u> caused thousands of deaths.*

fast, *adjective*: moving with speed; advancing or progressing rapidly.

  ✦ *Junko is a very <u>fast</u> runner. She ran a 10K marathon in under 35 minutes.*

fast, *noun*: a period of time without eating; *verb*: to go without eating.

  ✦ *Michi went on a <u>fast</u> for three days.*

feast, *noun*: a large, excellent meal; an abundance of well-prepared food.

  ✦ *My mother prepared a delicious <u>feast</u> to celebrate my graduation.*

gluttony, *noun*: an excess of eating or drinking; greedy or excessive indulgence.

  ✦ *<u>Gluttony</u> can be a dangerous habit for overweight people with diabetes.*

savor, *verb*: to really enjoy; to experience satisfaction and pleasure in taste or smell.

  ✦ *I eat very slowly in order to <u>savor</u> my favorite food.*

vegetarian, *noun*: one who eats no meat; a meatless diet.

  ✦ *As a <u>vegetarian</u>, Kazuko doesn't eat meat.*

ACTIVITY 3: ASK MORE QUESTIONS

A. Select five words from the vocabulary list and write a question for each word. Remember to start your question with a question word (Who, What, Where, When, Why, How, Is, Are, Do, Did, Does, etc.). You will also want to end each question with a question mark (?). Underline each vocabulary word.

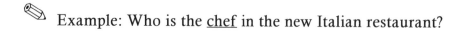 Example: Who is the <u>chef</u> in the new Italian restaurant?

1. ....

2. ....

3. ....

4. ....

5. ....

B. Take turns asking and answering questions with your partner.

ACTIVITY 4: PHOTOGRAPHS TO START CONVERSATIONS

Photographs capture moments, inform viewers, and start conversations. In small groups, examine the photograph and discuss the questions that follow.

Japanese tourists are often surprised at the huge portions served in the United States. The Sidewalk Café, a famous beachside American restaurant in Venice Beach, California, serves many international tourists.

1. What is happening in this picture?

2. What kind of food do you like to eat when you travel?

3. How much food is too much food for you?

4. Can you think of some fast food restaurants that change their menu to adjust to local tastes?

5. What foods do you think show up in Japanese fast food restaurants that appeal to tourists?

6. With your partner, can you list the last five fast food restaurants you ate in?

ACTIVITY 5: PARAPHRASING PROVERBS

A. We have many expressions about food. Read the following expressions, and discuss them with your partner. What do they mean? Circle your favorites. Explain your choices.

1. Eggs and promises are easily broken. —Japanese

Meaning: ....

....

2. Laughter is brightest where the food is best. —Irish

Meaning: ....

....

3. Eat less, live longer. —German

Meaning: ....

....

4. One must eat to live, not live to eat. —Spanish

Meaning: ....

....

5. A bath refreshes the body; tea refreshes the mind. —Japanese

Meaning: ....

....

B. Can you add another proverb about food, drinks, and meals?

1. ....

ACTIVITY 6: PRONUNCIATION PRACTICE

You can speak English with a distinctly Japanese accent and still be clearly understood. However, reducing confusing sounds can greatly improve your communication with English speakers and help to eliminate confusion in your English conversations.

"W" AND "U"

While Japanese has the sound "wa," there are no other vowel combinations that go with the "w" sound. However, in English, there are many "w + vowel" combinations. To make up for this, the Japanese often try to replace the "w" sound with the "u" sound in order to make an approximate match. Unfortunately, this is very confusing for many native speakers.

Some words create no problems: Wine, for example, is very easy because the pronunciation matches the Japanese "wa-in." Wood, however, cannot be understood when pronounced as "uddo."

To make the "w" sound, begin as you would with pronouncing "wa" and change the shape of your mouth as you leave the sound.

WORD / NOT A WORD

Take turns reading the words from your lists below. The first words in the shaded boxes are NOT real words. They have been written in "*Katakana* English." The word in parentheses (...) is the real word. After you read each word, have your partner guess if you are saying a real word or not.

Partner A		Partner B
wood		wolf
uuru (wool)		welcome
wink		uddo (wood)
wave		wafer
urufu (wolf)	Use your hand to cover your partner's list.	ueebu (wave)
ueedo (wade)		ueeru (well)
west		uinku (wink)
uefaa (wafer)		wool
uerukomu (welcome)		wade
well		uesuto (west)

Note: This activity contained many words that do not exist, but that Japanese speakers might say. Be careful with "w" words as they can cause confusion.

ACTIVITY 7: THE CONVERSATION CONTINUES

Let's continue to explore eating and drinking with one or two classmates. Use complete sentences to respond.

1. What is your favorite restaurant? Do you go there more than twice a month?

2. How often do you eat at a fast food restaurant? Which is your favorite?

3. Are American fast food chains popular in Japan? What do Japanese like about American fast food?

4. Do all members of your family eat dinner together? Who cooks? Who serves the food?

5. In Japan, what special foods or drinks are associated with weddings?

6. Do you prefer coffee or green tea?

7. What happens to your eyes or nose when you eat too much wasabi?

8. Have you ever fasted? Why? Were you very hungry after skipping two meals?

9. Do you eat hamburgers and pizza with a knife and fork? Or do you use your hands?

10. Do you have your own cup and your own chopsticks that you use at your family's house?

11. Have you ever tried to go on a diet to lose weight? What did you do?

12. Do you eat local cuisine (Kobe beef in Kobe) when you travel?

13. Do you think restaurants should ban smoking? What about bars? Why?

14. Do you usually read food labels? Why?

15. Does your family share recipes? Which recipe would you like to share?

ACTIVITY 8: DISCUSSING QUOTATIONS

Take turns reading these quotations out loud and discuss them with your partner. Do you agree with the quotation? Disagree? Why? Afterwards, pick a favorite quotation by circling the number and explain your choice. Remember to give a reason or example.

1. "The eating of meat extinguishes the seed of great compassion."
   —*Buddha, Siddhartha Gautama (563–483 B.C.E.), philosopher*
   ☐ Agree   ☐ Disagree
   Why? ....

2. "Tea ... is a religion of the art of life."
   —*Okakura Kakuzo (1862–1913), Japanese scholar*
   ☐ Agree   ☐ Disagree
   Why? ....

3. "Understand, when you eat meat, that something did die. You have an obligation to value it."

—*Anthony Bourdain (1956–), American chef and TV star*

☐ Agree   ☐ Disagree

Why? ....

4. "Live. Love. Eat."

—*Wolfgang Puck (1949–), American celebrity chef*

☐ Agree   ☐ Disagree

Why? ....

5. "If it's beautifully arranged on the plate, you know someone's fingers have been all over it."

—*Julia Child (1912–2004), American chef and author*

☐ Agree   ☐ Disagree

Why? ....

6. "More die in the United States of too much food than of too little."

—*John Kenneth Galbraith (1908–2006), American ambassador and economist*

☐ Agree   ☐ Disagree

Why? ....

7. "Making sushi is an art, and experience is everything."

—*Nobu Matsuhisa (1949–), Japanese celebrity chef and restaurant owner*

☐ Agree   ☐ Disagree

Why? ....

8. "Every time I look into his eyes, I just want to take the ice cream or whatever I've got in my hand and rub it into his face. That's how much I like him."

—*Banana Yoshimoto (1964–), Japanese author*

☐ Agree   ☐ Disagree

Why? ....

9. "You can't just eat good food. You've got to talk about it too. And you've got to talk about it to somebody who understands that kind of food."

—*Kurt Vonnegut (1922–2007), American author*

☐ Agree   ☐ Disagree

Why? ....

10. "Japanese chefs believe our soul goes into our knives once we start using them. You wouldn't put your soul in a dishwasher!"

    —*Masaharu Morimoto (1955–), Japanese chef*

    ☐ Agree   ☐ Disagree

    Why? ....

My favorite quote was: ....

....

Why? ....

ACTIVITY 9: TELL ME ABOUT JAPAN ... IN ENGLISH

People want to know about Japan and Japanese culture. Next time you travel abroad or meet a foreigner, you can tell them about Japan in English.

FAST FOOD!

What do you eat when you want to eat something tasty yet also filling? In the United States, we often eat hamburgers for a tasty, filling, and affordable meal. You can add fries, a salad, or fruit for a full meal.

In Japan, *donburi* (rice bowl dish) seems as common as hamburgers are in the U.S. Both have many variations from region to region and remain popular with young and old.

Can you list three types of *donburi* you like? Have you ever made your own unique *donburi*? What was it like?

1. ....

2. ....

3. ....

Would you count *donburi* by itself as a whole meal, or does it need other sides? What would you add with *donburi* to make it a complete meal? List three choices.

1. ....

2. ....

3. ....

ROLE PLAY

Night Out at a Fancy Restaurant in Miami

Find online reviews of upscale restaurants in Miami, Florida, for a fun night out with a group of friends. Use the reviews to select a restaurant.

Role Play Preparation: Asking Questions

Eating out can be fun and satisfying, especially if ordering in English. What are three typical questions to ask a waiter at your selected restaurant?

1. ....
2. ....
3. ....

What are three questions you might ask a friend at dinner?

1. ....
2. ....
3. ....

Role Play: Accidents Happen!

Everybody wants to have a good time when they go out, but sometimes bad things happen to good people—even in nice restaurants!

Let's imagine this situation: It's very busy at a fashionable Miami restaurant on Saturday night. A new waiter, Pedro, has just started. He's very nervous. Two friends arrive for dinner, and they want to talk. At the restaurant, everybody wants to have a good time, but accidents do happen.

What will happen? Who are the friends?
What do they want to talk about?
Which Miami restaurant are they going to?
Who is the waiter?
Why is the restaurant so busy?
What accident will happen?
What will happen next?

> **"You can say the service is good when it isn't intrusive, but comes straightaway when required."**
>
> —*Nobu Matsuhisa (1949–), Japanese celebrity chef*

Can you create a fun skit? Answer the questions and act in your own play. Have fun.

SEARCH and SHARE

Choosing a Local Restaurant

Student Name: .... Date: ....

Class: .... Teacher: ....

Can you recommend a good place for dinner around here? Find and share a positive review for a local restaurant you like. Pick a favorite local restaurant, do some research, and pick the best review—in Japanese or in English. Use this worksheet to tell us about the review. Remember restaurant reviews should provide examples and details. Tell us about a special restaurant—in English—and help us find a place to eat delicious food.

Restaurant: .... Location: ....

Review: .... Reviewer: ....

1. Why did you pick this review?

2. How does the reviewer describe the restaurant? What kind of food does it serve?

3. When was the review written?

4. What do you know about the reviewer?

5. What does the reviewer say about the restaurant's atmosphere?

6. How did the reviewer describe the restaurant's service?

7. What did the reviewer eat?

8. What was the best part of the restaurant review?

9. Does the reviewer recommend the restaurant? Why?

10. How often have you been to the restaurant? What makes this restaurant special?

> ## "One man's meat is another man's poison."
> —*Latin proverb*

5

EXPLORING DAILY HABITS

VOCABULARY WARM-UP

Which words do you already know? Underline them, and circle the words you are unsure about. Then review your answers with a partner.

bargain	consumer	curious	discipline	habit
impulsive	lifestyle	oversleep	routine	schedule

ACTIVITY 1: SHARING EXPERIENCES

Do you know your own habits? Share stories about your habits and find out more about your partner too.

1. How many hours of sleep do you usually get? Are you an "early bird" or a "night owl"?

2. What time do you usually get up in the morning? Do you use the alarm on your phone to wake you up?

3. Do you usually jump out of bed, or do you press the snooze button?

4. Can you describe your morning habits? Are you in a hurry? Do you have time to eat breakfast, walk your dog, or read the newspaper?

5. Do you have any bad habits? Can you tell me one bad habit?

6. Can you think of a few habits people often want to make or break for their New Year's resolutions?

7. How do you try to develop healthy habits?

8. What do you usually eat for breakfast? Do you eat on the run or do you skip breakfast?

9. How did you come to school today? Did you arrive by bus, by car, by bike, or on foot?

10. How long is your daily commute to work or school?

11. What are your shopping habits for clothes? Do you tend to buy the same type of clothes?

12. Can you describe your daily schedule? Do you have a favorite time of day?

13. What was your daily schedule like five years ago? How is it different now?

14. What tasks or chores have you put off or postponed?

15. Do you do many things at the last minute? Do you like to procrastinate? Why?

ACTIVITY 2: EXPANDING VOCABULARY

Look at the definitions and example sentences that follow. Do the definitions match what you and your partner expected in the vocabulary warm-up list? If not, what is different?

---

bargain, *noun*: a good buy for the price.

+ *Bargains are easy to find in Shinsaibashi.*

bargain, *verb*: to try to buy an item at a cheaper price.

+ *I bargain with the sellers when I shop for bargains in the markets.*

consumer, *noun*: a person who buys products or services.

+ *Consumers like bargains; they like to buy quality products at low prices.*

curious, *adjective*: an active desire to learn or know about things.

+ *Kaz has a curious mind and browses the Internet for hours.*

---

curious, *adjective*: strange or unusual.

    ✦ *Jill had a <u>curious</u> habit of stroking her eyebrow when she talked to me.*

discipline, *noun*: behavior that follows strict rules.

    ✦ *The young man learned <u>discipline</u> when he joined the large accounting firm.*

disciplined, *adjective*: following a strict routine.

    ✦ *You need a more <u>disciplined</u> approach to pass that difficult chemistry exam.*

habit, *noun*: repeated course of action developed over time; settled routine.

    ✦ *By <u>habit</u> and self-discipline, the old farmer got up before dawn and worked until sunset.*

impulsive, *adjective*: act suddenly without thought.

    ✦ *Kara was <u>impulsive</u> and bought three brand-name handbags in Ginza.*

lifestyle, *noun*: the way a person leads their life.

    ✦ *Yuki's <u>lifestyle</u> includes shopping during the day and going out with friends at night.*

oversleep, *verb*: to sleep late; to fail to wake up on time.

    ✦ *I set two alarm clocks so I wouldn't <u>oversleep</u> and miss an important school exam.*

routine, *noun*: the same activity or pattern; established way of acting.

    ✦ *My mother follows the same <u>routine</u> every day: she wakes up at five in the morning and goes to sleep at ten at night.*

routine, *adjective*: usual; typical.

    ✦ *The <u>routine</u> medical check-up confirmed the patient was healthy.*

schedule, *noun*: a timetable or a series of events.

    ✦ *My <u>schedule</u> is very full. Can we meet next week?*

schedule, *verb*: to make appointments.

    ✦ *Can I <u>schedule</u> a tour of the university campus next week?*

ACTIVITY 3: ASK MORE QUESTIONS

A. Select five words from the vocabulary list and write a question for each word. Remember to start your question with a question word (Who, What, Where, When, Why, How, Is, Are, Do, Did, Does, etc.). You will also want to end each question with a question mark (?). Underline each vocabulary word.

✐ Example: What is your <u>schedule</u> for next semester?

1. ....

2. ....

3. ....

4. ....

5. ....

B. Take turns asking and answering questions with your partner or group members.

ACTIVITY 4: PHOTOGRAPHS TO START CONVERSATIONS

Photographs capture moments, inform viewers, and start conversations. In small groups, examine the photograph and discuss the questions that follow.

1. Can you describe this picture?

2. What are these firefighters doing? Why?

3. What do you think the firefighter in the front is feeling? Why?

4. What are some reasons why people might want to be firefighters?

5. Do you think firemen* have unusual sleeping habits? Do you think sleeping is a necessity, a hobby, or a luxury?

6. What habits should firefighters develop to stay calm in stressful situations?

* firemen is the traditional term for firefighters.

Culture Corner: Changing Work Titles

Many professions were traditionally only open to men. As women have gained greater rights and society has become more equal, the titles used for many professions have changed. It is important, however, to recognize both traditional and modern terms for various professions. We recommend the use of modern terms that show women can hold these important positions too.

Traditional	Modern
fireman	firefighter
chairman	chair
businessman	business professional

Can you think of some other examples?

Traditional	Modern

ACTIVITY 5: PARAPHRASING PROVERBS

A. Read the following proverbs, and discuss them with your partner. What do they mean? Circle your favorites. Explain your choices.

1. Character can be built on daily routine. —Japanese

Meaning: ....

....

2. Habits are first cobwebs, then cables. —Spanish

Meaning: ....

....

3. Love makes marriage possible, and habit makes it endurable. —American

Meaning: ....

....

4. The fool in a hurry drinks his tea with chopsticks. —Chinese

Meaning: ....

....

5. The day you decide to do it is your lucky day. —Japanese

Meaning: ....

....

B. Can you add another proverb related to daily choices and habits?

1. ....

ACTIVITY 6: PRONUNCIATION PRACTICE

You can speak English with a distinctly Japanese accent and still be clearly understood. However, reducing confusing sounds can greatly improve your communication with English speakers and help to eliminate confusion in your English conversations.

"S" AND "SH"

In Chapter 3 we looked at "s" sounds compared to "th". Here we will focus on the tricky issue of "s" and "sh". When you see a word written with an "s" instead of an "sh", it is always pronounced with only the "s" sound. Many Japanese people find this pattern confusing because the "s" is followed by an "i" or "ee" sound in Japanese, which is pronounced as a "sh" sound.

As mentioned above, the problem with "s" and "sh" is usually not the ability to make the sound, but to choose the right one when speaking. Therefore, we need to pay careful attention to the vowels that follow the sound.

CHARADES

In this fun activity, Partner A will choose any word from the "sh" column. Partner B will listen and use physical gestures—but NO voice—to "act out" the word. If Partner B answers correctly, both students will switch roles. If Partner B guesses incorrectly, Partner A will choose another word and Partner B will be the "actor" again.

"s" words	"sh" words
sea	she
seal	shell
seat	sheet
single	shingle
sin	shin
sip	ship
seep	sheep
sift	shift
sill	shill
scene	sheen

Making Sure We Are Understood

Sometimes we want to make sure we are understood by other people. There are several phrases we can use to do this in English. The first three expressions are usually heard in conversations, and the last three expressions are more common for teachers or speakers to use during presentations.

CHECKING THAT SOMEONE HAS UNDERSTOOD YOU

Conversations	Presentations
Was I clear?	Are you with me?
Do you know what I mean?	Do you have questions about this topic?
Is that clear?	Should we review together?
Can you understand that?	Are we on the same page?
Sorry, was that clear enough?	Can I answer some questions?

ACTIVITY 7: THE CONVERSATION CONTINUES

Let's continue to explore daily habits with one or two classmates. Use complete sentences to respond.

1. Do you look for bargains when shopping? Do you compare store prices to online prices when you shop? Why or why not?

2. What are your TV viewing habits? Do you always watch certain shows? Which ones?

3. How many hours a day do you use the computer? Smartphone? What do you usually do online?

4. How often do you check for email or text messages? When do you send them? When is the last time you sent a postcard or letter by "snail mail"?

5. Do you prefer to send traditional text messages, or do you like using a special app? Why?

6. Do you consider smoking a bad habit? Why? What diseases do you associate with smoking?

7. In what ways are you self-disciplined? Are you naturally self-disciplined, or do you have to work at it?

8. Are you sometimes lazy? When? In what ways?

9. Do you tend to see the glass as half-full or half-empty? Are you more of an optimist or a pessimist? Why?

10. Do you find daily life hectic? Can you give some examples?

11. What are some dangerous or unhealthy habits?

12. What are some of your healthier habits?

13. What are some of your less healthy habits?

14. How do your habits compare to those of your parents? Your friends?

15. Can you describe what you would like your typical day to be like in five years?

ACTIVITY 8: DISCUSSING QUOTATIONS

Take turns reading these quotations out loud and discuss them with your partner. Do you agree with the quotation? Disagree? Why? Afterwards, pick a favorite quotation by circling the number and explain your choice. Remember to give a reason or example.

1. "You can only fight the way you practice."
   —*Musashi Miyamoto (1584–1685), Japanese warrior and author of* The Book of Five Rings
   ☐ Agree   ☐ Disagree
   Why? ....

2. "Men's natures are alike; it is their habits that separate them."
   —*Confucius (551–479 B.C.E.), Chinese philosopher*
   ☐ Agree   ☐ Disagree
   Why? ....

3. "We are what we repeatedly do. Excellence, then, is not an act, but a habit."
   —*Aristotle (384–322 B.C.E.), Ancient Greek philosopher*
   ☐ Agree   ☐ Disagree
   Why? ....

4. "The more things you do outside of your norm, the more ideas you get exposed to, the more people you get exposed to. I think that's interesting."

—*Masi Oka (1974–), Japanese-American actor and special effects artist*

☐ Agree   ☐ Disagree

Why? ....

5. "Any man who reads too much and uses his own brain too little, falls into lazy habits of thinking."

—*Albert Einstein (1879–1955), American Nobel Prize-winning scientist*

☐ Agree   ☐ Disagree

Why? ....

6. "Habits change into character."

—*Ovid (43 B.C.E.–17 C.E.), Ancient Roman poet*

☐ Agree   ☐ Disagree

Why? ....

7. "The chains of habit are too weak to be felt until they are too strong to be broken."

—*Dr. Samuel Johnson (1709–1784), English author*

☐ Agree   ☐ Disagree

Why? ....

8. "Notice the difference between what happens when a man says to himself, 'I have failed three times,' and what happens when he says, 'I'm a failure.'"

—*S. I. Hayakawa (1906–1992), Japanese-American linguist and U.S. Senator*

☐ Agree   ☐ Disagree

Why? ....

9. "The unfortunate thing about this world is that good habits are so much easier to give up than bad ones."

—*W. Somerset Maugham (1874–1965), English novelist*

☐ Agree   ☐ Disagree

Why? ....

10. "My process is thinking, thinking, and thinking—thinking about my stories for a long time."

—*Hayao Miyazaki (1941–), Japanese director*

☐ Agree   ☐ Disagree

Why? ....

My favorite quote was: ....

....

Why? ....

ACTIVITY 9: TELL ME ABOUT JAPAN ... IN ENGLISH

People want to know about Japan and Japanese culture. Next time you travel abroad or meet a foreigner, you can tell them about Japan in English.

AGEMONO

Japanese food is very well known for being healthy, but many Japanese people love fried foods! From *Kara-age* to *Kushi-katsu*, fried food is everywhere in Japan. Some Japanese even have a habit of eating fried food for lunch and dinner. What do you know about Japan's love of *agemono*?

For example: Tempura was introduced to the Japanese by the Portuguese in the mid-sixteenth century.

Think of three more things visitors to Japan might want to know about *agemono*. How can you explain these ideas?

1. ....

2. ....

3. ....

With your partner, can you ask and answer three questions about *agemono*?

For example: Do you think of *agemono* as a Japanese food or a Western food? Why?

1Q. ....
A. ....

2Q. ....
A. ....

3Q. ....
A. ....

WHAT IS THE 5W/H FILTER?

What is the 5W/H filter? **Who** can use this technique? **Where** can English students use the 5W/H filter in daily conversations? **When** can Japanese speakers use this method? **Why** do many journalists and managers use the 5W/H filter in their work? **How** can the 5W/H filter keep conversations going?

Some English students will already be familiar with the idea of 5W/H as the general question words: Who, What, Where, When, Why, and How. This checklist approach encourages speakers to bring these questions directly back into the conversation. Can you guess how it works?

When you are asked a question, practice running the answer through the "5W/H Filter." Make sure you answer at least two of the question words to provide details. Let's look at an example of a typical casual conversation.

Nick: What did you do this weekend?
Nobu: I went shopping.
Nick: That's good.
Nobu: ...
Nick: See you later.

This short conversation might be pleasant, but it wasn't too informative.

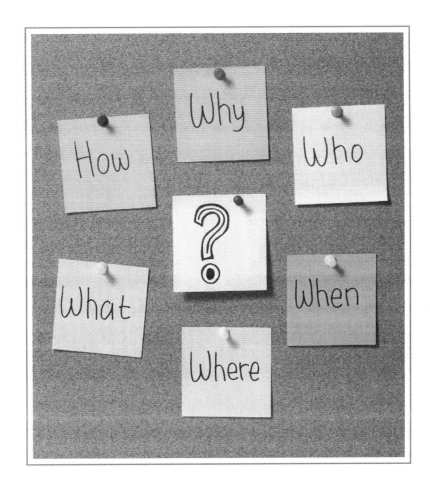

Now let's run the conversation through the 5W/H filter.

Question: "What did you do this weekend?"

Filter: What: Went shopping

   Who: With my sister

   When: Saturday

   Where: At the outlet

   Why: We were looking for a present for our brother's birthday.

   How: We rode our bicycles.

With the filter in place, Nobu has several places to take the conversation. When Nobu chooses to share at least three of the filtered answers, it's much more interesting and compelling. Nick may then continue the conversation in several directions.

Let's take a look at how the conversation might go:

Nick: What did you do this weekend?

Nobu: I went shopping at the outlet on Saturday with my sister. We were looking for a present for our brother's birthday.

Nick: Oh, really? How old will your brother be?

OR

Nick: How is the outlet? I haven't been there yet.

OR

Nick: I didn't know you had a sister! How many people are in your family?

By providing details, Nobu and Nick learn more and share more about their lives and activities. They can also maintain longer, better conversations. If they want, Nobu and Nick can cycle through the 5W/H filter again, and the two can talk for as long as they want! The good friends will learn more about each other and their friendship can become even stronger.

PROBLEM-SOLUTION WORKSHEET

The English proverb "two heads are better than one" is often true. Solving problems can frequently be difficult. Working with your partners, focus on a problem—at school, at work, or in the local city—and find a reasonable solution together. Follow this widely used problem-solution method. You can also use the 5W/H filter in this exercise. Sharing detailed, precise information is an important skill in academic and professional situations. Be ready to share your process and conclusions with your other classmates. You might even be asked to give a short presentation too!

DEFINE THE PROBLEM

1. What's the background?
2. What's the problem?
3. What are some short-term effects resulting from this problem?
4. What are some long-term effects resulting from this problem?

FIND THE BEST SOLUTION

1. What is a possible solution?

    a. What would be an advantage of this solution?
    b. What would be a disadvantage?

2. What is another possible solution?

    a. What would be an advantage of this solution?
    b. What would be a disadvantage?

3. Is there a third possible solution?

    a. What would be an advantage of this solution?
    b. What would be a disadvantage?

> **"In the middle of a difficulty lies an opportunity."**
> —*Albert Einstein (1879–1955),* Time *Magazine Man of the 20th Century*

Of these solutions, which do you think is the best? Provide three reasons.

1. ....

2. ....

3. ....

SEARCH and SHARE

How Do You Spend Your Time?

Student Name: .... Date: ....

Class: .... Teacher: ....

Enter the amount of time you spend on each of the following activities on a typical weekday. Use your best estimate or guess for each category.

	hours / minutes
sleeping	_____ : _____
eating and drinking	_____ : _____
housework/cleaning up	_____ : _____
attending classes	_____ : _____
working at a job	_____ : _____
commuting/driving	_____ : _____
playing sports and exercising	_____ : _____
using your cell phone	_____ : _____
watching TV	_____ : _____
attending religious services/praying	_____ : _____
socializing and relaxing	_____ : _____

For any of the above activities, would you say that you spend more or less time on it compared to other students in your class?

> **"All the treasures of the earth cannot bring back one lost moment."**
> —*French proverb*

6

BEING YOURSELF

VOCABULARY WARM-UP

Which words do you already know? Underline them, and circle the words you are unsure about. Then review your answers with a partner.

accurate	character	flexible	generous	nurture
optimist	patient	pessimist	rigid	talkative

ACTIVITY 1: SHARING EXPERIENCES

From consulting charts and reading palms to taking personality tests and reading self-help books, people love to describe themselves. Self-awareness is also an important skill when applying to universities, during job interviews, and going on dates.

1. Which three adjectives describe your personality?

2. Are you shy or outgoing? When are you most outgoing? When are you most shy?

3. Are you adventurous or cautious? In what ways?

4. Are you usually patient or impatient? Can you give an example?

5. Are you quiet or talkative? When are you most talkative? When do you think it is good to be quiet?

6. What are some groups you belong to? Would you call yourself a leader or a follower? Why?

7. Are you generous or selfish? Can you give an example?

8. In what ways are you rigid? In what ways are you flexible?

9. In what ways are you traditional? In what ways are you modern?

10. If pessimistic is a 1 and optimistic is a 10, what would your number be on the scale? Why did you decide on that number?

11. What is one of your favorite words in English? Why? What about in Japanese? Why?

12. Who do you resemble in your family? In what ways?

13. Which color would you use to describe your personality? Why?

14. Which animal would you use to describe yourself? A tiger or a mouse? A cat or a dog? A rabbit or a turtle? Another animal? Why?

15. Have you ever taken a personality test from a magazine or a website? What did it say? What did you think of the test?

ACTIVITY 2: EXPANDING VOCABULARY

Look at the definitions and example sentences that follow. Do the definitions match what you and your partner expected in the vocabulary warm-up list? If not, what is different?

---

accurate, *adjective*: correct; getting the facts right.

+ *Scientists, engineers, and doctors must be <u>accurate</u>.*

character, *noun*: inner-self, personality, and values.

+ *Emi showed her <u>character</u> at work when she stayed at the company until after midnight to finish the important project.*

character, *noun*: a figure in fiction or theater.

+ *Oliver Twist is one of my favorite <u>characters</u> in English literature.*

---

flexible, *adjective*: loose; bending; willing to change.

   ✦ *Mari is <u>flexible</u> and can work either Saturday or Sunday.*

generous, *adjective*: giving; sharing with others.

   ✦ *A good sister is <u>generous</u> with her time and helps her family.*

nurture, *verb*: to take care of another; to care for or help someone in need.

   ✦ *Good teachers <u>nurture</u> their students and help them succeed.*

patient, *adjective*: able to wait calmly; not in a hurry.

   ✦ *A <u>patient</u> person can calmly wait for a late bus.*

patient, *noun*: a person receiving medical treatment.

   ✦ *The doctor gave some powerful medicine to her sick <u>patient</u>.*

optimist, *noun*: someone who sees the positive side of life and believes things will get better.

   ✦ *Even when life is difficult, Chiyo is an <u>optimist</u> and sees the glass as half-full.*

pessimist, *noun*: one who has a negative view of life and thinks things will get worse.

   ✦ *Junichiro is a <u>pessimist</u> who sees the glass as half-empty and expects bad things to happen.*

rigid, *adjective*: unwilling to change; inflexible.

   ✦ *Sho is so <u>rigid</u> that he will not listen to his brother, his friends, or anyone else.*

talkative, *adjective*: verbal; engages in constant or nonstop conversation.

   ✦ *Hiro becomes <u>talkative</u> when he relaxes with his friends.*

ACTIVITY 3: ASK MORE QUESTIONS

A. Select five words from the vocabulary list and write a question for each word. Remember to start your question with a question word (Who, What, Where, When, Why, How, Is, Are, Do, Did, Does, etc.). You will also want to end each question with a question mark (?). Underline each vocabulary word.

✎ Example: What are the benefits of being an <u>optimist</u>? A <u>pessimist</u>?

1. ....

2. ....

3. ....

4. ....

5. ....

B. Take turns asking and answering questions with your partner or group members.

ACTIVITY 4: PHOTOGRAPHS TO START CONVERSATIONS

Photographs capture moments, inform viewers, and start conversations. In small groups, examine the photograph and discuss the questions that follow.

1. Can you describe this picture?

2. Why do you think this young woman is smiling?

3. Are there social pressures to get married? What are the best reasons to marry? The worst?

4. Which type of wedding would you prefer?

5. What are some advantages of a traditional Japanese wedding?

6. What are some advantages of a modern Japanese wedding?

ACTIVITY 5: PARAPHRASING PROVERBS

A. Read the following proverbs, and discuss them with your partner. What do they mean? Circle your favorites. Explain your choices.

1. Laughter brings happiness. —Japanese

Meaning: ....

....

2. A smile will gain you ten more years of life. —Chinese

Meaning: ....

....

3. Trust yourself. —American

Meaning: ....

....

4. You can't keep a good man down. —American

Meaning: ....

....

5. One who smiles rather than rages is always the stronger. —Japanese

Meaning: ....

....

B. Can you add another proverb about character or advice?

1. ....

ACTIVITY 6: PRONUNCIATION PRACTICE

You can speak English with a distinctly Japanese accent and still be clearly understood. However, reducing confusing sounds can greatly improve your communication with English speakers and help to eliminate confusion in your English conversations.

"A" AND "UH"

Learning how to pronounce vowels correctly can really help listeners understand you better when speaking English. As you may know, the Japanese language has a very limited number of vowel sounds. Therefore, many native Japanese speakers sometimes find it challenging to master the wide variety of vowel sounds in English.

In this lesson, we will look at the difference between the "a" sound in a word like *cat* and the "uh" sound in a word like *cut.* To make the "a" sound, you have to drop your tongue, tighten your jaw, and pull your mouth back in a half-smile.

The "uh" sound is the most common sound in English. Relax every muscle in your face and throat, and let the sound come out. That is the "uh" sound. You might find looking in a mirror helpful for this exercise.

DO WE MATCH?

In the following activity, Student A will read #1 from their list and Student B will read #1 from their list. They will listen carefully to each other and see if they are saying the same word or different words. Remember to fold the page in two, and cover your partner's word list.

	Student A			Student B
1	bat		1	but
2	cup		2	cup
3	match		3	munch
4	fun	Fold the page in two, and cover your partner's word list.	4	fan
5	bag		5	bag
6	track		6	truck
7	slum		7	slam
8	mad		8	mad
9	stub		9	stub
10	cat		10	cut

Did you find all your matching answers? For the words that were the same, how do you pronounce the word with the other vowel sound? For example, if you both had the word "mad," the other word would be "mud." With practice, you will it easier to distinguish between these two important vowel sounds.

ACTIVITY 7: THE CONVERSATION CONTINUES

Let's continue to explore being yourself with one or two classmates. Use complete sentences to respond.

1. Do you think our personalities are set when we are born? Why?

2. Can we change our personalities? How?

3. Do you think opposites attract? Why?

4. Which three words would you use to describe your best friend's personality?

5. How are your personalities similar? How are your personalities different?

6. Are you primarily an extrovert or an introvert? Why do you think so?

7. Some cultures define personality in terms of the elements. Would you say you are primarily air, water, fire, or earth? Explain your choice.

8. Which three qualities do you think of as feminine?

9. Which three qualities do you think of as masculine?

10. If you had been born in another country, do you think your personality would be different? How?

11. Can growing up in poverty influence someone's personality? How?

12. Would being born in extreme wealth influence your personality? How?

13. What are you grateful for in your life? Why?

14. What is the difference between personality and character?

15. What are your best qualities? Why?

ACTIVITY 8: DISCUSSING QUOTATIONS

Take turns reading these quotations out loud and discuss them with your partner. Do you agree with the quotation? Disagree? Why? Afterwards, pick a favorite quotation by circling the number and explain your choice. Remember to give a reason or example.

1. "Even bigger than Japan is the inside of your head."

    —*Natsume Soseki (1867–1916), Japanese novelist*

    ☐ Agree   ☐ Disagree

    Why? ....

2. "Know thyself."

    —*Socrates (470–399 B.C.E.), Greek philosopher*

    ☐ Agree   ☐ Disagree

    Why? ....

3. "This above all: To thine own self be true."

    —*William Shakespeare (1564–1616), English playwright*

    ☐ Agree   ☐ Disagree

    Why? ....

4. "Character is much easier kept than recovered."

    —*Thomas Paine (1737–1809), American writer*

    ☐ Agree   ☐ Disagree

    Why? ....

5. "In everyone's life, at some time, our inner fire goes out. It is then burst into flame by an encounter with another human being."

    —*Albert Schweitzer (1875–1965), French doctor and 1952 Nobel Peace Prize winner*

    ☐ Agree   ☐ Disagree

    Why? ....

6. "Man's main task in life is to give birth to himself, to become what he potentially is. The most important product of his effort is his own personality."

    —*Erich Fromm (1900–1980), German-American psychologist*

    ☐ Agree   ☐ Disagree

    Why? ....

7. "Generous people are rarely mentally ill people."

    —Karl Menninger (1893–1990), American psychiatrist

    ☐ Agree   ☐ Disagree

    Why? ....

8. "The easiest kind of relationship for me is with ten thousand people. The hardest is with one."

    —Joan Baez (1941–), American singer

    ☐ Agree   ☐ Disagree

    Why? ....

9. "Dwell in possibility."

    —Emily Dickinson (1830–1886), American poet

    ☐ Agree   ☐ Disagree

    Why? ....

10. "I knew I must try to forget the pain."

    —Shun Fujimoto (1950–), 1976 Olympic Gold Medalist

    ☐ Agree   ☐ Disagree

    Why? ....

My favorite quote was: ....

....

Why? ....

ACTIVITY 9: TELL ME ABOUT JAPAN ... IN ENGLISH

People want to know about Japan and Japanese culture. Next time you travel abroad or meet a foreigner, you can tell them about Japan in English.

ANIME

Anime is a very popular form of entertainment in Japan, but did you know that it is very popular overseas among young people? Why do you think anime has become such a major part of our global pop culture? What do you know about anime? For example:

Anime is a Japanese word that comes from the English word "animation." Think of three more details visitors to Japan might want to know about anime. How can you explain these ideas?

1. ....

2. ....

3. ....

With your partner, can you ask and answer three questions about anime?

For example: What is the most popular anime in Japan?

1Q. ....

A. ....

2Q. ....

A. ....

3Q. ....

A. ....

SEARCH and SHARE

Always Be Yourself

Student Name: .... Date: ....

Class: .... Teacher: ....

For better or for worse, many Americans often pride themselves on their individualism. The mass media often reinforce this idea in entertainment and school. Find a video about being yourself on YouTube.com or another video-sharing site.

1. What is the video or series segment about?

2. Can you describe one or two of the people or characters?

3. Did the main person or character face a problem? What was it?

4. What was the main idea of the video?

5. What was the most interesting part for you? Why?

6. Write five new vocabulary words, idioms, or expressions related to the topic.

   a.

   b.

   c.

   d.

   e.

7. Do you think "being yourself" is always a good idea? Why? Why not?

8. How would you rate the video on a scale of 1–5, with 5 being the highest? Why?

> **"Be yourself. Everyone else is already taken."**
> —*Oscar Wilde (1856–1900), Irish playwright*

7

MAKING AND KEEPING FRIENDS

VOCABULARY WARM-UP

Which words do you already know? Underline them, and circle the words you are unsure about. Then review your answers with a partner.

assist	betray	buddy	crisis	depend on
dependable	drift	roommate	support	supportive

ACTIVITY 1: SHARING EXPERIENCES

We all want good friends. Some people like to have just a few; some people like to have many. How does one make good friends? Share your ideas about friendship with your partner.

1. Did you have a best friend when you were eight years old? Who was it?

2. What did you do together? Can you describe your best friend?

3. Who was your best friend when you were 14 years old? What did you do together?

4. Are you still friends with the best friends of your youth?

5. Why do best friends sometimes drift apart?

6. What are some tips for keeping a friendship strong?

7. Who is your best friend now? How did you meet your best friend?

8. What activities do you do with your best friend? What makes this friendship special?

9. What do you and your best friend have in common?

10. How are you and your best friend different?

11. In your opinion, are there rules for a friendship? What are they?

12. Do you think you are a good friend to others? In what ways?

13. Do you think friends should loan each other money? Why or why not?

14. What do you like to do with your friends? Where do you like to go?

15. Which of your friends would make good roommates? Why?

ACTIVITY 2: EXPANDING VOCABULARY

Look at the definitions and example sentences that follow. Do the definitions match what you and your partner expected in the vocabulary warm-up list? If not, what is different?

---

assist, *verb*: to help.

   ✦ *My friends <u>assisted</u> me in cleaning up the house after the party.*

betray, *verb*: to violate a trust; to harm or be disloyal.

   ✦ *Kim would never <u>betray</u> me, so I trusted her with my secret.*

buddy, *noun*: a good friend; someone you are close with.

   ✦ *My <u>buddy</u> can get us the tickets to the concert.*

crisis, *noun*: an emergency situation; a critical time that requires decisive action.

   ✦ *The economic <u>crisis</u> caused many workers to lose their jobs and countless stores to close.*

---

depend on, *verb*: to count on; to rely on.

- ✦ *Children <u>depend on</u> their parents for love, protection, and financial support.*

dependable, *adjective*: loyal; reliable.

- ✦ *She is <u>dependable</u>; you can count on her help during this difficult time.*

drift apart, *verb*: to slowly separate; to grow distant.

- ✦ *They began to <u>drift apart</u> when he moved to Hokkaido.*

roommate, *noun*: someone you live with; a person who shares a house or apartment with you.

- ✦ *I have two amazing <u>roommates</u>. One is from America, and the other one is from Australia.*

support, *verb*: to give help; to assist; to recommend; to make stronger.

- ✦ *She <u>supported</u> her best friend during a very hard time.*

supportive, *adjective*: helpful; encouraging.

- ✦ *My mother is very <u>supportive</u> of my plans to study abroad in Canada.*

ACTIVITY 3: ASK MORE QUESTIONS

A. Select five words from the vocabulary list and write a question for each word. Remember to start your question with a question word (Who, What, Where, When, Why, How, Is, Are, Do, Did, Does, etc.). You will also want to end each question with a question mark (?). Underline each vocabulary word.

✎ Example: How do your friends <u>support</u> you?

1. ....
2. ....
3. ....
4. ....
5. ....

B. Take turns asking and answering questions with your partner or group members.

ACTIVITY 4: PHOTOGRAPHS TO START CONVERSATIONS

Photographs capture moments, inform viewers, and start conversations. In small groups, examine the photograph and discuss the questions that follow.

This couple got married at Santa Monica Beach in California. What do you think inspired this wedding photo?

1. Describe the picture.
2. Do you think you have to be best friends to marry your partner?
3. What are some tips to help couples remain close friends?
4. Do you believe the phrase "opposites attract" is true? Why?
5. What do you like about this photo?
6. What do you think makes a good marriage?

ACTIVITY 5: PARAPHRASING PROVERBS

A. Read the following proverbs, and discuss them with your partner. What do they mean? Circle your favorites. Explain your choices.

1. Absent friends get further away every day. —Japanese

Meaning: ....

....

2. Fate chooses your relatives; you choose your friends. —French

Meaning: ....

....

3. Do not protect yourself by a fence, but rather by your friends. —Czech

Meaning: ....

....

4. Lend money to a good friend, and you will lose the money as well as your friend.
   —Korean

Meaning: ....

....

5. When the character of a man is not clear to you, look at his friends. —Japanese

Meaning: ....

....

B. Can you add another proverb about friends?

1. ....

ACTIVITY 6: PRONUNCIATION PRACTICE

You can speak English with a distinctly Japanese accent and still be clearly understood. However, reducing confusing sounds can greatly improve your communication with English speakers and help to eliminate confusion in your English conversations.

FINAL "D" AND FINAL "DOE"

Because Japanese words almost always end in a vowel sound, many Japanese English-language learners make the common mistake of adding a vowel sound to the end of English words. Over the next few chapters, we will look at a number of these common mistakes. We could even say that these are "good mistakes" in a way because they are logical. Still, these mistakes only become "good mistakes" when we learn from them.

Words that end in a "d" are often given the Japanese "do" sound, which in English sounds like "doe."

While there is a voiced sound with "d", it is very short and cut off almost immediately. The voiced part is more similar to the "uh" sound we learned in Chapter 7 than the "o" sound.

Practice the following words. Repeat them until your partner is satisfied that you are using the correct pronunciation. If you're not sure, ask your English teacher.

We DO say:	We DO NOT say:
add	a-ddo
Holland	Holland-do
brand	bran-do
bread	bre-ddo
blend	blen-do
found	foun-do
bead	bea-do
bed	be-ddo
second	secon-do
red	re-ddo

This pronunciation problem is very common with proper names and places. Be careful. Many students who are a little bit familiar with this rule tend to cut off the "o" sound on words that should include it. In the United States, there are many cities and towns with names of Spanish origin that end in the "o" sound.

+ Orland**o**, Florida
+ Sacrament**o**, California
+ Chimay**o**, New Mexico

ACTIVITY 7: THE CONVERSATION CONTINUE

Let's continue to explore making and keeping friends with one or two classmates. Use complete sentences to respond.

1. How do you meet new friends? Do you have any tips for making friends?

2. Why do friends often form in crisis situations?

3. How do you keep in touch with friends?

4. How would your friendships change without smartphones and computers?

5. How do you use a search engine (Yahoo, Google, etc.)? What do you research?

6. Do you think people of the opposite sex can be friends? Why? How about roommates? Can they be buddies?

7. Do you know any married partners who are also best friends? If so, why do you think that relationship works?

8. What was the most memorable time you had with your best friend?

9. Do you think it is fair to judge people by their friends? Why?

10. What are some things you prefer to do with a group of friends, rather than one?

11. What unites you? In what ways do you depend on one another?

12. What are some good reasons for ending a friendship?

13. Can you think of classic stories about true friendship?

14. How do you deepen friendships?

15. Can you share three tips for keeping a friendship strong?

ACTIVITY 8: DISCUSSING QUOTATIONS

Take turns reading these quotations out loud and discuss them with your partner. Do you agree with the quotation? Disagree? Why? Afterwards, pick a favorite quotation by circling the number and explain your choice. Remember to give a reason or example.

1. "In joy or sadness, flowers are our friends."
    —*Okakura Kakuzo (1862–1913), Japanese scholar*

    ☐ Agree   ☐ Disagree
    Why? ....

2. "Have no friends not equal to yourself."
   —*Confucius (551–479 B.C.E.), Chinese philosopher*
   ☐ Agree   ☐ Disagree
   Why? ....

3. "The shifts of fortune test the reliability of friends."
   —*Cicero (106–43 B.C.E.), Roman statesman*
   ☐ Agree   ☐ Disagree
   Why? ....

4. "It is more shameful to distrust our friends than to be deceived by them."
   —*François de La Rochefoucauld (1613–1680), French philosopher*
   ☐ Agree   ☐ Disagree
   Why? ....

5. "Animals are such agreeable friends; they ask no questions, they pass no criticisms."
   —*George Eliot / Mary Ann Evans (1819–1880), English novelist*
   ☐ Agree   ☐ Disagree
   Why? ....

6. "It is easier to forgive an enemy than to forgive a friend."
   —*William Blake (1757–1827), English poet*
   ☐ Agree   ☐ Disagree
   Why? ....

7. "The only way to have a friend is to be one."
   —*Ralph Waldo Emerson (1803–1882), American poet*
   ☐ Agree   ☐ Disagree
   Why? ....

8. "It's the friends you can call up at 4 a.m. that matter."
   —*Marlene Dietrich (1901–1992), German-American actress and singer*
   ☐ Agree   ☐ Disagree
   Why? ....

9. "Even where friendships are concerned, it takes me a long time to trust people."
   —*Namie Amuro (1977–), Japanese singer*
   ☐ Agree   ☐ Disagree
   Why? ....

10. "Don't walk behind me, I may not lead. Don't walk in front of me, I may not follow. Just walk beside me and be my friend."
—*Albert Camus (1913–1960), French author/journalist, 1957 Nobel Prize winner*

☐ Agree   ☐ Disagree

Why? ....

My favorite quote was: ....

....

Why? ....

ACTIVITY 9: TELL ME ABOUT JAPAN ... IN ENGLISH

People want to know about Japan and Japanese culture. Next time you travel abroad or meet a foreigner, you can tell them about Japan in English.

The *senpai / kohai* relationship is very important in Japan, especially in the school system, but this relationship is not very important in most Western countries. What do you know about the *senpai / kohai* system? For example: Even if a *kohai* gets a better job and more success, the *senpai / kohai* relationship does not change.

Think of three more things visitors to Japan might want to know about the *senpai / kohai* system. How can you explain these ideas?

1. ....

2. ....

3. ....

With your partner, can you ask and answer three questions about *senpais* and *kohais*?

For example: Who is an important *senpai* in your life?

1Q. ....

A. ....

2Q. ....

A. ....

3Q. ....

A. ....

Culture Corner: Make vs. Do

What do you do? What do you make?

What's the difference between "make" and "do"? What expressions use "do" and which expressions use "make"? These simple words can cause a lot of confusion.

English has many different idioms and expressions that use these two hardworking, common verbs. Here is a quick guide that helps clarify the difference between these two important, but small words.

Look at some common expressions with "**do**":

- You **do the dishes** every day.
- I **do some chores** during the week.
- We **do our work** in an office.
- You **do homework** for English class.
- We **do exercises** to stay healthy.
- **Do your best** on exams.
- Please **do the report** on time.
- We will **do it over** when required.

Do is used to describe an activity that you have to do, often over and over again. For instance, we "**do the dishes**" and "**do the laundry**" many times. "**Do**" also contains an element of duty, obligation, and responsibility.

Now, take a look at some expressions with "**make**":

- You **make art** for fun.
- You **make lunch** at noon.
- You **make drawings** in art class.
- You **make decisions** every day.
- You **make plans** for the future.
- Your **make reservations** for dinner.
- You **make mistakes** on an exam.
- You **make progress** when you study hard.
- You **make money** at work.
- You **make friends** at school.
- You **make time for** your family and friends.

"**Make**" is used to describe a creative activity or something you choose to do. You choose, for instance, to **make** plans, **make** friends, and **make** decisions. You have choices.

Why do we say "**make dinner**" if we have to do it over and over? Perhaps because cooking is seen more as a creative activity than a necessary chore. But cleaning the table and cleaning the dishes are just chores, so we say "**do the table**" and "**do the dishes**." That's also why Americans say "**make money**" instead of "do money." Making money is seen as both a creative activity and a choice. Learning this expression shows how the United States remains a strong consumer culture—even in the most common expressions.

Sometimes we forget how much cultural information can be contained in short sayings and everyday idioms. Americans will often use the verb "make" in a way that might seem strange to English students. Many English students, for example, note that they don't choose to "**make mistakes**" on their exams! Still, English students usually "**make a decision**" to "**do their best**" and "**make progress**" in learning a confusing language.

What do you do during a typical week? Write three sentences describing your habits. Use some of the idioms with "do."

1.

2.

3.

What do you like to do in your free time? Write three sentences describing your habits. Use some of the idioms with "make."

1.

2.

3.

Can you think of some other expressions or idioms that use the words "do" and "make"? Work with your partner and come up with five more English expressions that use "do" or "make."

1.

2.

3.

4.

5.

_____ / 10

Student Name: .... Date: ....

Class: .... Teacher: ....

Have you heard about TED (Technology, Entertainment, Design) talks yet? These can be fascinating, surprising, and sometimes controversial talks by global experts in many disciplines. The presenters give highly personal presentations that address many important and interesting topics in short, engaging talks. The exceptional pace of change—technological, social, and economic—remains a constant TED theme.

Give yourself time to explore TED.com, browsing by topic or speaker. Find a short video on a topic of particular interest to you that you can recommend. Watch it twice or more, answer the following questions, and be prepared to share your recommendation. You can also read the subtitles if that will help you better understand the presentation.

Title: .... Location: ....

Speaker: .... Date: ....

1. Why did you choose this TED talk?

2. How did the presentation begin?

3. What is the theme of the talk?

4. What did you learn from this TED talk?

5. What did the speaker want to accomplish?

6. What do you believe is the best thing about this TED talk? Why?

7. How did the speaker connect to his audience? (humor, visual aids, etc.)

8. Did the speaker convince you? Why?

9. How would you rate this TED talk on a scale of 1–5, with 5 being the highest?

10. Why are you recommending this particular talk to your classmates?

"Make change your friend."

—_William (Bill) Jefferson Clinton (1946–), 42nd U.S. President_

8

SHARING PET PEEVES

VOCABULARY WARM-UP

Which words do you already know? Underline them, and circle the words you are unsure about. Then review your answers with a partner.

annoy	bother	courtesy	impolite	litter
obnoxious	offended	pet peeve	polite	profanity

ACTIVITY 1: SHARING EXPERIENCES

Sometimes things annoy us, and that's okay. Share your complaints and pet peeves with your partner. Talking and sharing our frustrations and complaints can sometimes help us feel better in difficult situations.

1. What annoys you? Do you have any pet peeves at home or at work?

2. What are some of the things people do that you find impolite? Can you give a couple of examples?

3. How can salespeople be annoying? Can you give some examples?

4. Have you ever had phone problems? How did you respond? Do technical "glitches" bother you?

5. Do you know many people who share your pet peeves? Which ones?

6. What sounds bother you? What do you feel when you hear them?

7. What are some sounds you find annoying? Burping? Sneezing? Blowing one's nose in public?

8. What are some things you find annoying about the way people talk?

9. What is litter? Have you seen any litterbugs? Where does litter bother you the most? Do you pick it up?

10. What do you consider bad cell phone manners? Why?

11. When, or where, do you most often see people get stressed? Can you give an example?

12. What behavior by a neighbor might be considered annoying?

13. How do you feel about aggressive people? Is there a difference between assertive and aggressive?

14. What is something people do that you find mean, wrong, or immoral?

15. Is there something else you can't stand? Do you have any more pet peeves?

ACTIVITY 2: EXPANDING VOCABULARY

Look at the definitions and example sentences that follow. Do the definitions match what you and your partner expected in the vocabulary warm-up list? If not, what is different?

---

annoy, *verb*: to disturb or irritate.

+ *Loud traffic noises <u>annoy</u> me when I'm trying to sleep.*

bother, *verb*: to annoy; to disrupt or disturb; to make one feel bad.

+ *I'm sorry to <u>bother</u> you. Could you tell me how to get to the train station?*

courtesy, *noun*: a kind or polite act; politeness.

+ *It's a common <u>courtesy</u> to hold a door open for others.*

impolite, *adjective*: using poor behavior; rude.

+ *It's <u>impolite</u> to talk while eating.*

---

litter, *noun*: trash that can be seen on the street; garbage on the ground.

   ✦ *Please put your <u>litter</u> in the trash can.*

litter, *noun*: a number of dogs or cats born at the same time to the same mother.

   ✦ *My dog gave birth to a <u>litter</u> of six puppies.*

obnoxious, *adjective*: extremely annoying; bothersome.

   ✦ *The <u>obnoxious</u> boy kept singing the same song over and over and over.*

offended, *adjective*: feeling upset or insulted.

   ✦ *She felt <u>offended</u> when her friend said she was a bad mother.*

pet peeve, *noun*: something that annoys or irritates a person.

   ✦ *My biggest <u>pet peeve</u> is people talking on their cell phone or texting while driving.*

polite, *adjective*: using good manners; respectful.

   ✦ *Sachiko was <u>polite</u> when she opened the door for the elderly woman.*

profanity, *noun*: a bad word; offensive language.

   ✦ *Many countries prohibit, or ban, <u>profanity</u> on radio and TV during a broadcast.*

ACTIVITY 3: ASK MORE QUESTIONS

A. Select five words from the vocabulary list and write a question for each word. Remember to start your question with a question word (Who, What, Where, When, Why, How, Is, Are, Do, Did, Does, etc.). You will also want to end each question with a question mark (?). Underline each vocabulary word.

✎ Example: What sounds <u>annoy</u> you?

1. ....

2. ....

3. ....

4. ....

5. ....

B. Take turns asking and answering questions with your partner or group members.

ACTIVITY 4: PHOTOGRAPHS TO START CONVERSATIONS

Photographs capture moments, inform viewers, and start conversations. In small groups, examine the photograph and discuss the questions that follow.

1. Can you describe this picture?
2. Do you know anybody who has allergies? How do allergies annoy people?
3. Do you think people should wear a mask when they have the flu or a cold? Why?
4. Do you consider pollen a pollutant? Why or why not?
5. What are some problems that air pollution can cause?
6. What are some causes of air pollution?

ACTIVITY 5: PARAPHRASING PROVERBS

A. Read the following proverbs, and discuss them with your partner. What do they mean? Circle your favorites. Explain your choices.

1. A short temper is a disadvantage. —Japanese

Meaning: ....
....

2. Hatred is as blind as love. —Irish

Meaning: ....
....

3. Control yourself: remember anger is only one letter short of danger. —American

Meaning: ....

....

4. Love makes a good eye squint. —English

Meaning: ....

....

5. The reputation of a thousand years may be determined by the conduct of one hour. —Japanese

Meaning: ....

....

B. Can you add another proverb about handling anger?

1. ....

ACTIVITY 6: PRONUNCIATION PRACTICE

You can speak English with a distinctly Japanese accent and still be clearly understood. However, reducing confusing sounds can greatly improve your communication with English speakers and help to eliminate confusion in your conversations.

FINAL "J" AND FINAL "JI"

As we explored in the last chapter, many Japanese students tend to add an "o" sound when the word ends in a "d". This pattern usually doesn't create too much confusion. However, when words end in the "j" sound, it can often create some communication problems because many Japanese speakers will convert the "d" into a "ji" sound. In English, many words (happy, silly, funny) that end in the "i" sound are adjectives.

When words end with a "j" sound, such as hedge, we need to be very careful not to add a final sound. For example, we do not want to convert "hedge" to "hedgy." It should also be noted that several English words that have this sound —age, page, wage —do not have an adjective form. As a result, some English speakers may not understand your words.

No "i" sound (noun)	"i" sound (adjective)
hedge	hedgy
range	rangy
edge	edgy
ridge	ridgy
stage	stagy
ledge	ledgy
cage	cagey
cabbage	cabbagey
dodge	dodgy
fringe	fringy

Check out the following sentences. Using the lists above, can you pick the correct word and form to fill in the blanks? Say them out loud with your partner.

1. The first time the famous actress Miwa stepped on the ...., her life was changed forever.

2. What is in this soup? Did you put .... in it?

3. When I was younger, I loved playing .... ball.

4. There are many pigeons on the .... of that building.

5. Nicolas Cage, a famous American actor, is known for portraying .... characters.

ACTIVITY 7: THE CONVERSATION CONTINUES

Let's continue to explore pet peeves with one or two classmates. Use complete sentences to respond.

1. What table manners or eating styles make you frown?

2. What pet peeve might an impatient person have?

3. Where do you think adults generally act their worst? Why do you think that is?

4. How does a polite child act? How does a rude child behave?

5. Where do people learn good manners? What are good manners?

6. Can you describe a polite boss? Have you ever worked for a difficult boss? What was he or she like?

7. How have coworkers or classmates annoyed you? How did you handle the situation?

8. How have you handled working with rude customers? Are you able to keep your cool?

9. Do foul language and profanity offend you? When?

10. What obnoxious behavior upsets you?

11. Have you ever walked out of a movie? Were you bored, offended, or tired? Why?

12. Which personality traits do you find extremely disagreeable? Why?

13. Is there one thing that annoyed you ten years ago that does not annoy you today? What pet peeve have you outgrown?

14. Do you have some tips on how to keep calm when angry?

15. What is the opposite of having a pet peeve? Can you give an example?

ACTIVITY 8: DISCUSSING QUOTATIONS

Take turns reading these quotations out loud and discuss them with your partner. Do you agree with the quotation? Disagree? Why? Afterwards, pick a favorite quotation by circling the number and explain your choice. Remember to give a reason or example.

1. "Holding on to anger is like grasping a hot coal with the intent of throwing it at someone else; you are the one who gets burned."
   —Buddha (563–483 B.C.E.), Indian spiritual teacher
   ☐ Agree   ☐ Disagree
   Why? ....

2. "Good manners are made up of petty sacrifices."
   —Ralph Waldo Emerson (1803–1882), American essayist
   ☐ Agree   ☐ Disagree
   Why? ....

3. "Someone who butts in when you're talking and smugly provides the ending herself. Indeed anyone who butts in, be they child or adult, is most infuriating."

—*Sei Shōnagon (966–1017?), Japanese author of* The Pillow Book

☐ Agree ☐ Disagree

Why? ....

4. "Anger makes dull men witty, but it keeps them poor."

—*Francis Bacon (1561–1626), English author and philosopher*

☐ Agree ☐ Disagree

Why? ....

5. "When you're down and out, something always turns up—usually the noses of your friends."

—*Orson Welles (1915–1985), American actor and director*

☐ Agree ☐ Disagree

Why? ....

6. "Always forgive your enemies—nothing annoys them so much."

—*Oscar Wilde (1854–1900), Irish poet, novelist, dramatist*

☐ Agree ☐ Disagree

Why? ....

7. "One thing I hate in movies is when the camera starts circling around the characters. I find that totally fake."

—*Takeshi Kitano (1947–), Japanese filmmaker, comedian, actor, screenwriter*

☐ Agree ☐ Disagree

Why? ....

8. "People ask you for criticism, but they only want praise."

—*W. Somerset Maugham (1874–1965), English novelist*

☐ Agree ☐ Disagree

Why? ....

9. "When angry, count to ten before you speak. If very angry, count to one hundred."

—*Thomas Jefferson (1743–1826), American founding father, 3rd U.S. President and author*

☐ Agree ☐ Disagree

Why? ....

10. "I may be making fashion in the sense of craftsmanship, but I hate the world of fashion."

—*Yohji Yamamoto (1943–), Japanese award-winning fashion designer*

☐ Agree   ☐ Disagree

Why? ....

My favorite quote was: ....

....

Why? ....

ACTIVITY 9: TELL ME ABOUT JAPAN ... IN ENGLISH

People want to know about Japan and Japanese culture. Next time you travel abroad or meet a foreigner, you can tell them about Japan in English.

The Japanese train system is very famous for being efficient, clean, and crowded. What do you know about Japanese trains?

For example: The *Shinkansen* is also known as the "Bullet Train." In 1962, it was the first train to go 200 kilometers an hour. It also set a world record of 603 km/h in April 2015. It's the world's busiest high-speed rail line.

Think of three more things visitors to Japan might want to know about Japanese trains. How can you explain these ideas?

1. ....

2. ....

3. ....

With your partner, can you ask and answer three questions about Japanese trains?

For example: Some trains have a special "women only" carriage. Do you think this is a good idea?

1Q. ....

A. ....

2Q. ....

A. ....

3Q. ....

A. ....

TIPS FOR GIVING A PRODUCT REVIEW

You have probably bought hundreds of items as a consumer. You have looked at and considered thousands more. You can't buy everything; you have to pick and choose the products that fit you and your lifestyle. Also, almost everyone has a budget.

Product reviews play an important role in our consumer culture. We have many choices, and we see many advertisements. Companies want our attention and our money. In turn, smart shoppers want to make informed consumer choices.

Product reviews are very popular today. Consumers can easily share their experiences and opinions—positive or negative—online. Strong product reviews combine both facts and opinions while offering revealing details. Reading labels and searching online can provide valuable information.

A strong product review should include:

- a description of the product

- the way the product is used

- the cost of the product

- a comparison with other, similar products

- a combination of facts and opinions

- a recommendation to buy or not buy the product

- a reason for your recommendation

- a rating on a scale of 1–5, with 5 being the highest

Your experience and opinion matter too. Therefore, you can use your personal experiences. You also, however, want to show your classmates that you did some additional research by citing a source. You might use the following phrases in your product review:

In a consumer review on ....,

According to a survey ....,

A 2015 article praised the latest model for ....

Expert .... described the product as ....

Citing other research and giving sources will also make your product review more convincing. Creating a persuasive product review is a practical life skill, but it can also be fun to share our opinions and help other consumers make better choices.

SEARCH and SHARE

Give a Product Review

Student Name: .... Date: ....

Class: .... Teacher: ....

Product reviews are increasingly popular, and you can find many places to share reviews. For your next class, pick a consumer product to review. Do some research online about the product. Find at least two sources of information. Then fill in this worksheet, and create a product review to share with your classmates.

Product: .... Company: ....

Sources: .... Date: ....

1. Do you own the product?

2. What is the purpose of the product?

3. Who is the target audience for this product? Who usually uses it?

4. How is the product used?

5. What does the product cost?

6. What competitors does the product have?

7. What are some disadvantages of the product?

8. Are there some possible dangers or misuses of the product?

9. What did you learn during your research about this product?

10. Do you recommend this product for your classmates? Why?

11. How do you rate the product on a scale of 1–5, with 5 being the highest? Why?

> **"The customer is always right."**
> —*American proverb*

9

TAKING PHOTOGRAPHS

VOCABULARY WARM-UP

Which words do you already know? Underline them, and circle the words you are unsure about. Then review your answers with a partner.

compose	crisp	expose	film	model
photojournalism	photoshop	portrait	shutterbug	store

ACTIVITY 1: SHARING EXPERIENCES

Almost everybody in Japan and the United States seems to have a camera. In the past, a camera was an expensive consumer product that far fewer folks could afford. Over the decades, camera technology has dramatically changed, and it appears almost everyone enjoys taking photographs. We can find photographs in many places and spaces. Chat with your conversation partner about photography and its role in our lives and the modern world.

1. What was the first photo you took? Where were you?

2. Do you have a favorite picture of yourself as a child? What do you remember about the experience?

3. What kind of photographs do you like? Why?

4. In the event of a catastrophe such as a fire or earthquake, which photographs would you take with you? Why are they important to you?

5. What might cause someone to feel embarrassed about a picture? (They were blinking, eyes closed, etc.) What do you suggest someone do with these photographs?

6. What are portraits? What makes a good portrait? What are some problems that might cause a "bad" portrait?

7. Is photojournalism more powerful for you than a written article? Why or why not?

8. Have you ever taken a photo of someone famous? Who? Which famous person would you like to take a photo with?

9. Are you a shutterbug? Do you take a lot of photos? Why?

10. How do you store your photos? In an album? On a computer? On a disk? On a smartphone?

11. Do you have any friends who compose their photos very well? What do they photograph?

12. Have you ever felt sad or even cried because of a photograph? Can you describe the photograph?

13. How is photography used in advertising? What makes an ad memorable for you?

14. How do photographs of models help sell products? Can you think of some famous models?

15. What do you think about fashion photos that have been altered or photoshopped? Why do you think there is controversy over the use of altered photographs of fashion models?

ACTIVITY 2: EXPANDING VOCABULARY

Look at the definitions and example sentences that follow. Do the definitions match what you and your partner expected in the vocabulary warm-up list? If not, what is different?

compose, *verb*: to organize parts to make a whole image, often in an artistic way.

 ✦ *Miho <u>composed</u> the photo carefully in order to see the cherry blossoms and Mt. Fuji.*

crisp, *adjective*: clean and clear with a high amount of detail.

 ✦ *The <u>crisp</u> photograph of the pyramids made Atsushi feel like he was back in Egypt.*

expose, *verb*: to let a certain amount of light inside the camera.

 ✦ *Satoshi <u>exposed</u> his picture for too long, so the picture is mostly white.*

film, *noun*: light-sensitive plastic used in traditional cameras.

 ✦ *While digital photography is much more popular these days, some people feel that <u>film</u> photography is more authentic.*

model, *noun*: a man or woman who is a standard or example for comparison.

 ✦ *Yuki became a successful fashion <u>model</u>.*

model, *verb*: to show or display something.

 ✦ *Yuki <u>models</u> beautiful Italian clothes in international fashion shows.*

photojournalism, *noun*: the practice of sharing the news through photographs.

 ✦ *His <u>photojournalism</u> documented a humanitarian crisis and won an award for the brave war photographer.*

photoshop, *verb*: to alter a digital photograph or other image, using an image-editing application.

 ✦ *Most magazine covers, such as* Elle, Frau, *and* Vogue, *are <u>photoshopped</u>.*

portrait, *noun*: an image of a person using only their head and shoulders.

 ✦ *As a wedding photographer, Rina learned to take beautiful <u>portraits</u>.*

shutterbug, *noun*: an amateur photographer, especially one who is greatly devoted to the hobby.

 ✦ *The number of <u>shutterbugs</u> has increased in the last decade.*

store, *verb used with object*: to put or retain (data) in a memory unit.

 ✦ *Nobu <u>stores</u> all his photos on an external hard drive.*

ACTIVITY 3: ASK MORE QUESTIONS

A. Select five words from the vocabulary list and write a question for each word. Remember to start your question with a question word (Who, What, Where, When, Why, How, Is, Are, Do, Did, Does, etc.). You will also want to end each question with a question mark (?). Underline each vocabulary word.

✎ Example: Would you rather go into photojournalism or fashion photography?

1. ....

2. ....

3. ....

4. ....

5. ....

B. Take turns asking and answering questions with your partner or group members.

ACTIVITY 4: PHOTOGRAPHS TO START CONVERSATIONS

Photographs capture moments, inform viewers, and start conversations. In small groups, examine the photograph and discuss the questions that follow.

1. Can you describe this picture?

2. How would you describe this girl?

3. Do you think she is passionate about photography? Why?

4. Would you ever get a tattoo? If yes, of what? If no, why not?

5. Sometimes Westerners with tattoos want to go to Japanese hot springs (*onsen*), but find they are not allowed. How would you explain the reasoning for this?

6. Does your opinion of people change if you see they have a tattoo? Why?

ACTIVITY 5: PARAPHRASING PROVERBS

A. Photography deals with light, sight, and vision. Black and white photography, with numerous shades of gray, can emphasize shapes, shadows, and contrasts. Some photographers still prefer to shoot in black and white. Read the following proverbs, and discuss them with your partner. What do they mean? Circle your favorites. Explain your choices.

1. Picture it! —American expression

Meaning: ....

....

2. Out of sight, out of mind. —English

Meaning: ....

....

3. Clicking with people is more important than clicking a shutter. —American

Meaning: ....

....

4. Seeing is believing. —English

Meaning: ....

....

5. A picture is worth a thousand words. —Advertising slogan

Meaning: ....

....

B. Can you think of another proverb about photography or the way we see things?

1. ....

Culture Corner:
Advertising Slogans

Like proverbs, advertising slogans are often short and direct. International companies spend huge amounts of money promoting their products and creating a memorable slogan. Nike, for instance, used the slogan "Just do it!" to build a strong connection to consumers. Camera companies have a history of effective marketing and advertising. Can you match these English language slogans with a Japanese company?

1. You don't have to be a Pro to shoot like a Pro.   A. Nikon

2. Change your lens, change your story.   B. Canon

3. Lose a hobby. Gain a passion.   C. Fuji Film

4. In this family, everyone is photogenic.   D. Pentax

5. In the heart of the image.   E. Sony

Can you name another advertising slogan for a photography or technology company?

....

....

ACTIVITY 6: PRONUNCIATION PRACTICE

You can speak English with a distinctly Japanese accent and still be clearly understood. However, reducing confusing sounds can greatly improve your communication with English speakers and help to eliminate confusion in your English conversations.

"SL" AND "SUL"

Much like the previous chapter, there are often issues when tricky letters like "s" and "l" are put together. Many Japanese speakers find it easier to mix them by putting a "u" between them, matching the Japanese "su" sound. This is not a natural sound in English, so let's work to eliminate the unnecessary vowel sound. The word "slam" can often become the word "sulam," which would be hard for many native English speakers to understand.

Make the "s" sound as you normally would, but instead of pursing your lips to make the "su" sound, lift your tongue to touch the ridge above your upper teeth. Then you can slide your tongue to make the next vowel sound.

WHICH IS RIGHT?

Try to say the following words correctly (with the "sl" pronunciation) three times and incorrectly (with the "sul" pronunciation) once. Try to mix up when you say the word incorrectly. Your partner will mark an X when they hear the incorrect version. Then switch roles.

"sl" word	1	2	3	4
slack				
slay				
slam				
slip				
sleep				
slimy				
slow				
slender				
slip				
slump				

ACTIVITY 7: THE CONVERSATION CONTINUES

Let's continue to explore taking photographs with one or two classmates. Use complete sentences to respond.

1. How have cameras changed? What are some settings on a camera? What's the difference between landscape and portrait mode?

2. What are paparazzi? Why are paparazzi controversial?

3. Within the last six months, which celebrities have been photographed quite a bit? Do you have a favorite celebrity photograph?

4. Do you think it's okay to take a photo of someone without their permission? Why or why not?

5. Can you describe a headshot? A group shot? A mugshot?

6. What do you like to take photographs of? Why do you take photographs?

7. What makes a good photograph? What makes a great photograph?

8. Which season of the year do you prefer to take photos? Why?

9. Where are some beautiful places in Japan to take stunning pictures?

10. What are your favorite travel pictures? Why?

11. What have you learned from your photographs?

12. What are some Japanese companies involved in photography and film industries? Why do you think Japan has been so successful in this field?

13. How would the world be different today without photography?

14. Do you carry photographs on your smartphone? Do you carry photographs in your wallet or purse?

15. Can you show me some of your favorite photographs?

ACTIVITY 8: DISCUSSING QUOTATIONS

Take turns reading these quotations out loud and discuss them with your partner. Do you agree with the quotation? Disagree? Why? Afterwards, pick a favorite quotation by circling the number and explain your choice. Remember to give a reason or example.

1. "You don't take a photograph; you make it."

   —*Ansel Adams (1902–1984), American photographer and naturalist*

   ☐ Agree ☐ Disagree

   Why? ....

2. "When you look at my pictures, you are seeing my life."

   —*Douglas Kirkland (1934–), American photographer*

   ☐ Agree ☐ Disagree

   Why? ....

3. "When you photograph people in color you photograph their clothes. But when you photograph people in black and white, you photograph their souls!"
   —*Dr. Ted Grant (1951–), Canadian photojournalist*

   ☐ Agree   ☐ Disagree

   Why? ....

4. "I came to realize that natural features in Japan, like the nature of its people, were extremely diversified and complex. I intended to investigate this conclusion with my own eyes."
   —*Hiroshi Hamaya (1915–1999), Japanese photographer*

   ☐ Agree   ☐ Disagree

   Why? ....

5. "The surreal exists within the real. Tireless experimentation with new photography leads to the creation of a new beauty."
   —*Kansuke Yamamoto (1914–1987), Japanese surrealist photographer*

   ☐ Agree   ☐ Disagree

   Why? ....

6. "A very subtle difference can make the picture or not."
   —*Annie Leibovitz (1949–), American photographer*

   ☐ Agree   ☐ Disagree

   Why? ....

7. "Light makes photography. Embrace light. Admire it. Love it. But above all, know light. Know it for all you are worth, and you will know the key to photography."
   —*George Eastman (1854–1932), American inventor and founder of Eastman Kodak*

   ☐ Agree   ☐ Disagree

   Why? ....

8. "Your first 10,000 photographs are your worst."
   —*Henri Cartier-Bresson (1908–2004), French photographer*

   ☐ Agree   ☐ Disagree

   Why? ....

9. "Character, like a photograph, develops in darkness."
   —*Yousuf Karsh (1908–2002), Canadian photographer*

   ☐ Agree   ☐ Disagree

   Why? ....

10. "Seeing is not enough; you have to feel what you photograph."
—*Andre Kertesz (1894–1985), American photographer*

☐ Agree ☐ Disagree

Why? ....

My favorite quote was: ....

....

Why? ....

ACTIVITY 9: TELL ME ABOUT JAPAN ... IN ENGLISH

People want to know about Japan and Japanese culture. Next time you travel abroad or meet a foreigner, you can tell them about Japan in English.

PHOTO BOOTHS – JAPANESE STYLE

This *purikura* was actually created online. The photo was uploaded and the writing was added as an effect. *Purikura*, short for *Purinto Kurabu* in Japan, has been popular since the mid-1990s. The postage stamp-sized pictures made in photo booths come with writing. *Purikura* has become a part of Japanese pop culture. If a foreigner were visiting you, where would you take them to try *purikura*?

For example: I would take a friend to try *purikura* in Sega World because there are many choices.

Discuss the following questions with your partner:

1. Do you remember the very first time you took a *purikura* photo?
2. Were you alone? Who were you with?
3. Do you still have your first *purikura*?
4. What is your favorite *purikura*?
5. What makes a wonderful *purikura*?

With your partner, can you ask and answer three questions about *purikura*?

For example: What makes *purikura* fun?

1Q. ....

A. ....

2Q. ....

A. ....

3Q. ....

A. ....

GRAMMAR REVIEW: CAN, MIGHT, SHOULD, MUST

Finish the sentences below in a way that reflects your opinion.

A good photograph can ....

A good photograph might ....

A good photograph should ....

A good photograph must ....

A good photographer can ....

A good photographer might ....

A good photographer should ....

A good photographer must ....

Culture Corner:
Street Photography, Paparazzi, and Manners

"I prowled the streets all day, feeling very strung up and ready to pounce, determined to 'trap' life—to preserve life in the act of living."
—*Henri Cartier-Bresson (1908–2004), French photographer*

Many people enjoy taking pictures of new places and strange sights while traveling. Some photographers also enjoy taking pictures of their own city and surroundings. Street photography focuses on taking pictures of people in public places without permission at "the decisive moment." Street photographs can capture dramatic, unplanned moments and document social situations. Street photography is also controversial.

People walking on a street, playing in a park, going to work on a train, or relaxing on a beach might be subjects for a street photographer. These natural images can be very powerful because they seem to capture a slice of reality. Eugene Atget, Henri Cartier-Bresson, Robert Frank, Harold Feinstein, and Daido Moriyama have won great praise for their candid street photography pictures.

Like street photographers, paparazzi can sometimes take natural pictures of celebrities and sell these photographs for money. Celebrities often want their privacy, but they have also chosen to become famous. Sometimes, however, paparazzi will take pictures of celebrities with their families and their children in public.

Yet the practice—and legality—of street photography continues to be debated. Different countries often have very different laws. Some people see street photography as free speech; other people see it as an invasion of privacy. Others think street photography should be legal, but consider it rude. What do you think?

1. Do you think paparazzi should take natural pictures of celebrities in their daily life? What about pictures of a celebrity's child?

2. Why do street photographers take pictures of people in public?

3. When do you think photographers should get permission to take photographs of people in public? Why?

4. How would getting permission before taking pictures change street photography?

SEARCH and SHARE

Documenting Moments in Time

Student Name: .... Date: ....

Class: .... Teacher: ....

Documentary photographs capture important moments in time. Visit the Library of Congress collection at www.loc.gov/pictures to find a special historical photograph that captures your imagination. Print it out and share it with your classmates.

Title: ....

Photographer: ....

Historical Context: .... Date: ....

1. Describe the photograph. What is going on?

2. How did the photographer compose his picture? Where are your eyes drawn?

3. What historical moment does it capture? Does it do it well?

4. Why do you think the photographer chose to take this picture?

5. Why did you choose this photograph?

6. What did you learn from it?

7. Do you think a photograph like this would still be taken today? Why? Why not?

8. On a scale of 1–5, with 5 being the highest, how would you rate the photograph? Why?

> **"There are always two people in every picture: the photographer and the viewer."**
> —Ansel Adams (1902–1984), American photographer and environmentalist

10

TALKING ABOUT MOVIES

VOCABULARY WARM-UP

Which words do you already know? Underline them, and circle the words you are unsure about. Then review your answers with a partner.

adapt	animation	blockbuster	cast	celebrity
director	famous	genre	popular	word of mouth

ACTIVITY 1: SHARING EXPERIENCES

Movies are a great topic of conversation when meeting new people. Everybody watches movies. Even people who claim they do not like movies have seen some, and talking about movies can be an easy way to get to know someone better. Talk with your partner and share your movie experiences.

1. Do you like to watch movies? Why?

2. Where do you usually watch movies? At home, on your computer, on a tablet, or in a theater? How often do you see movies?

3. How have you changed the way you watch movies? Do you rent at a store, or do you use the Internet, cable, or satellite?

4. Which movies have you seen more than once? Which movies have you seen more than twice? Why do you like these movies so much?

5. Do you own any movies? Which ones? Do you watch them repeatedly?

6. Have you figured out a way to see movies for free? What is your secret?

7. What do you like about the movie theater experience?

8. Do you have a favorite movie theater? Where do you prefer to sit?

9. Have you ever seen a celebrity or famous actor in person? Where did this happen? What was the celebrity doing?

10. Have you ever watched a movie in English without looking at the Japanese subtitles? How much did you understand?

11. Which Japanese movie do you like the most? Why?

12. Who is your favorite actor/actress? Why?

13. Have you ever acted in a play or a movie? Can you describe your experience?

14. What do you think would be difficult about being an actor or actress?

15. Have you ever watched a movie on your smartphone or tablet? If so, how is the experience different from watching a movie in a theater?

ACTIVITY 2: EXPANDING VOCABULARY

Look at the definitions and example sentences that follow. Do the definitions match what you and your partner expected in the vocabulary warm-up list? If not, what is different?

---

adapt, *verb*: to change; modify.

+ *Shakespeare's play* Romeo and Juliet *has been <u>adapted</u> many times into different films.*

animation, *noun*: a moving cartoon; a technique used to make drawings come alive.

+ My Neighbor Totoro *and* The Lion King *are two popular examples of <u>animation</u>.*

---

blockbuster, *noun*: a very popular movie, often with expensive special effects; *adjective*: pertaining to a major success.

+ *The blockbuster* Avatar, *which made over $1 billion, used fantastic special effects and inspired millions of movie fans.*

cast, *noun*: the actors in a play, show, or movie.

+ *The Harry Potter series has a great cast of British actors and actresses.*

cast, *verb*: to assign a role in a show.

+ *The director cast Rinko Kikuchi in the starring role.*

celebrity, *noun*: a famous person; a person who attracts media attention.

+ *The movie* Titanic *made the actress Kate Winslet a celebrity.*

director, *noun*: the person who tells the actors and crew what to do in the making of a film.

+ *Stephen Spielberg and Hayao Miyazaki are two of the world's best film directors.*

famous, *adjective*: well known; recognized by most people.

+ *Hollywood is famous for its movie stars and the film industry.*

genre, *noun*: a type of music, movie, book, or dance.

+ *Romantic comedies are Aoi's favorite genre, but her boyfriend prefers action movies.*

popular, *adjective*: well liked; regarded with affection.

+ The Avengers *was a very popular film worldwide.*

word of mouth, *noun*: the spread of an idea or cultural event from person to person; an informal or personal information network.

+ *The surprise movie of the summer became popular by word of mouth.*

ACTIVITY 3: ASK MORE QUESTIONS

A. Select five words from the vocabulary list and write a question for each word. Remember to start your question with a question word (Who, What, Where, When, Why, How, Is, Are, Do, Did, Does, etc.). You will also want to end each question with a question mark (?). Underline each vocabulary word.

✎ Example: Which <u>celebrity</u> would you like to meet?

1. ....
2. ....
3. ....
4. ....
5. ....

B. Take turns asking and answering questions with your partner or group members.

ACTIVITY 4: PHOTOGRAPHS TO START CONVERSATIONS

Photographs capture moments, inform viewers, and start conversations. In small groups, examine the photograph and discuss the questions that follow.

1. Can you describe this picture?
2. Have you ever seen this actor in English language movies? Which ones?
3. What is your favorite movie you have seen him in? Why?
4. Pick three adjectives to describe this famous actor.
5. Do you think it is difficult for Japanese actors to succeed in Western cinema? What are some obstacles?
6. Who are your favorite film stars? Why?

ACTIVITY 5: PARAPHRASING PROVERBS

A. What do these proverbs and sayings mean? Discuss them with your partner. Circle your favorite. Can you relate these proverbs and sayings about acting and the theater to movies?

1. Spectators see better than actors. —Persian

Meaning: ....

....

2. Perseverance brings success. —Dutch

Meaning: ....

....

3. Put faith in your own abilities, and not in the stars. —Japanese

Meaning: ....

....

4. It takes ten years to become an overnight success. —American

Meaning: ....

....

5. We're fools whether we dance or not, so we may as well dance. —Japanese

Meaning: ....

....

B. Can you add another proverb related to acting, performing, or the theater?

1. ....

ACTIVITY 6: PRONUNCIATION PRACTICE

You can speak English with a distinctly Japanese accent and still be clearly understood. However, reducing confusing sounds can greatly improve your communication with English speakers and help to eliminate confusion in English conversations.

FINAL "P" AND FINAL "PU/POO"

Many English words, as seen in previous chapters, end with consonants. Some Japanese speakers tend to sometimes add an extra vowel to these consonant endings. Unfortunately, this pronunciation pattern is hard to break. We can start with developing some awareness of the problem.

When English words end with a "p" sound, you do not need to make any voice. Simply pause the air behind your lips and quickly let out a small blast of air.

WORD / NOT A WORD

Take turns reading the words from your lists below. The first words in the shaded boxes are NOT real words. They have been written in "*Katakana* English." The second word in parentheses (...) is the real word. After you read each word, have your partner guess if you are saying a real English word or not. Do your best, and try to have some fun.

Partner A		Partner B
keepu (keep)		hip hop
sleep		cup
trap		trappu (trap)
peep		ship
cuppu (cup)	Use your hand to cover the other partner's word list.	sleepu (sleep)
yelp		peepu (peep)
hippu-hoppu (hip hop)		snap
shippu (ship)		syruppu (syrup)
syrup		keep
snappu (snap)		yelupu (yelp)

Note: This activity contains many words that do not exist, but which Japanese speakers might say.

ACTIVITY 7: THE CONVERSATION CONTINUES

Let's continue to explore movies with one or two classmates. Use complete sentences to respond.

1. Which genres of movies do you enjoy? Why?

2. What makes your favorite films so special or memorable?

3. Name a few movies you disliked. Why did you dislike them? Did you walk out on them in the theater or stop watching them at home?

4. Can you think of some books that have been adapted into movies? Did the adaptations work?

5. What was your favorite movie as a child? What movie did you like most as a teenager?

6. Who was your favorite movie star as a child? Why was this person your favorite? Do you still like this star?

7. Have you ever had a "crush" on a movie star?

8. Approximately how many movies do you watch in a year? Do you pay attention to word of mouth? How do you decide which movies you want to see?

9. Do you read movie reviews? Do you enjoy watching previews and movie trailers? Why?

10. Do you eat snacks when you watch movies at the movie theater? What do you eat?

11. Which actors, actresses, or directors would you like to have lunch with? What would you ask them?

12. Do you have any favorite directors? What is their filmmaking style?

13. In your opinion, what makes a good movie? Can you give an example?

14. What makes a great movie? Can you give an example of a great movie?

15. Which Japanese movies would you suggest to visitors planning to come to Japan? Why?

ACTIVITY 8: DISCUSSING QUOTATIONS

Take turns reading these quotations out loud and discuss them with your partner. Do you agree with the quotation? Disagree? Why? Afterwards, pick a favorite quotation by circling the number and explain your choice. Remember to give a reason or example.

1. "Japan does not understand very well that one of its proudest cultural achievements is in film."
   —*Akira Kurosawa (1910–1988), Japanese film director, producer, screenwriter, editor*
   ☐ Agree   ☐ Disagree
   Why? ....

2. "A celebrity is a person who works hard all his life to become well known, then wears dark glasses to avoid being recognized."
   —*Fred Allen (1894–1956), American comedian*
   ☐ Agree   ☐ Disagree
   Why? ....

3. "Animation offers a medium of storytelling and visual entertainment which can bring pleasure and information to people of all ages everywhere in the world."
   —*Walt Disney (1901–1966), American film producer and animator*
   ☐ Agree   ☐ Disagree
   Why? ....

4. "The day will come when everyone will be famous for fifteen minutes."
   —*Andy Warhol (1928–1987), American artist and filmmaker*
   ☐ Agree   ☐ Disagree
   Why? ....

5. "We need families to start taking more responsibility in understanding which movie is good for their children and which movie is not."
   —*Jet Li (1963–), Chinese actor and martial artist*
   ☐ Agree   ☐ Disagree
   Why? ....

6. "Movies are fun, but they're not a cure for cancer."
   —*Warren Beatty (1937–), American actor, director, and producer*
   ☐ Agree   ☐ Disagree
   Why? ....

7. "I don't want to limit myself. I want to keep doing all sorts of roles. I guess what lies behind this urge is the conviction that movies have changed my life."
   —*Rinko Kikuchi (1981–), Japanese film actress*
   ☐ Agree   ☐ Disagree
   Why? ....

8. "The success I have achieved in bodybuilding, motion pictures, and business would not have been possible without the generosity of the American people and the freedom here to pursue your dreams."
   —*Arnold Schwarzenegger (1947–), Austrian-American actor and former California governor*

   ☐ Agree   ☐ Disagree

   Why? ....

9. "The thing about filmmaking is I give it everything, that's why I work so hard. I always tell young actors to take charge. It's not that hard. Sign your own checks; be responsible."
   —*Tom Cruise (1962–), American actor and producer*

   ☐ Agree   ☐ Disagree

   Why? ....

10. "Life is like a movie; write your own ending. Keep believing."
    —*Jim Henson (1936–1990), American creator of the Muppets*

    ☐ Agree   ☐ Disagree

    Why? ....

My favorite quote was: ....

....

Why? ....

ACTIVITY 9: TELL ME ABOUT JAPAN ... IN ENGLISH

People want to know about Japan and Japanese culture. Next time you travel abroad or meet a foreigner, you can tell them about Japan in English.

> ### Culture Corner:
> ### Artists and Celebrities
>
> Akira Kurosawa is a prolific director who is respected all across the world. Which of his many films have you seen? When talking with cultured people from outside Japan, it may be a good idea to know about accomplished Japanese artists and celebrities. Many people think of Kurosawa as a master storyteller. Do you know why?

Akira Kurosawa (1910–1998) is one of the most popular film directors in the world. One of his famous statements is, "In a mad world, only the mad are sane." What do you know about Kurosawa?

For example: Akira Kurosawa directed the movie *The Seven Samurai* in 1954.

Think of three more facts visitors to Japan might want to know about Japanese movies. How can you explain these ideas?

1. ....

2. ....

3. ....

With your partner, ask and answer three questions about Japanese movies.

For example: What is the first Japanese film to win an Academy Award?

1Q. ....

A. ....

2Q. ....

A. ....

3Q. ....

A. ....

SEARCH and SHARE

Be a Movie Critic!

Student Name: .... Date: ....

Class: .... Teacher: ....

Can you recommend an excellent movie? Select one of your favorite movies, go to the website www.imdb.com, and research the selected film. Take notes. A strong movie review will combine both facts and opinions. Use this short worksheet to describe the movie and prepare to share your informed opinion with your classmates.

Title: .... Genre: ....

Director: .... Date: .... Length: ....

Actors/Actresses: ....

Awards? ....

How many times have you watched the movie? .... Where? ....

PLOT INFORMATION:

1. Where does the movie take place?

2. When does the movie take place?

3. Who are the main characters? Can you briefly describe them?

4. What happens in the movie?

5. What makes the movie interesting?

6. What is the best part? Why?

7. Does the movie surprise the audience? How? How could it be a better film?

8. How did you feel when the movie ended? Why?

9. Is there anything else you want to tell me about your favorite movie?

10. Who do you think would like this movie? Why?

11. Would you give a thumbs up (positive) or thumbs down (negative) review?

12. On a scale of 1–5 stars, with 5 being the highest, how do you rate this movie? Why?

> **"Every great film should seem new every time you see it."**
> —*Roger Ebert (1942–2013), American film critic*

11

LEARNING IN SCHOOL

VOCABULARY WARM-UP

Which words do you already know? Underline them, and circle the words you are unsure about. Then review your answers with a partner.

academic	adversity	bully	campus	dormitory
dress code	elementary	field trip	role model	tutor

ACTIVITY 1: SHARING EXPERIENCES

We have spent thousands of hours in schools, learned many skills, and collected numerous stories. Many people have their fondest memories from years in school. Share your school stories with a classmate.

1. Approximately how many hours a week were you in school? Did you go to school on Saturdays?

2. How did you usually get to school? Did you walk, take a bus, ride a bike, or use another form of transportation?

3. How long was your commute to high school?

4. How many students were in your class? What do you think is the perfect class size?

5. Did you have a favorite teacher? Why was this teacher your favorite?

6. What is your favorite memory about school?

7. Was there a dress code at your school? What were some of the other rules?

8. How would you describe your high school? Did you enjoy it?

9. Were your parents involved in your studies? How?

10. What does P.E. stand for? What was your favorite P.E. class?

11. Can you describe your high school? College?

12. Which was your least favorite class? Why?

13. What was your favorite class? Why?

14. How can you be a better student?

15. What does success in school mean to you? Why?

ACTIVITY 2: EXPANDING VOCABULARY

Look at the definitions and example sentences that follow. Do the definitions match what you and your partner expected in the vocabulary warm-up list? If not, what is different?

---

academic, *adjective*: educational; related to school.

+ *Academic life can continue after high school and college with online classes, evening classes, workshops, and continuing education classes.*

adversity, *noun*: harsh conditions; suffering; bad luck or hardship.

+ *Adversity can build character and make people stronger.*

bully, *noun*: an aggressive person who threatens weaker schoolmates or coworkers.

+ *Bullies must be disciplined by school authorities.*

---

bully, *verb*: to scare or threaten a person.

> ✦ *Tim <u>bullied</u> his classmates and later was expelled from school.*

campus, *noun*: school grounds.

> ✦ *The <u>campus</u> is the center of academic life at many universities.*

dress code, *noun*: rules on what clothing is allowed in school.

> ✦ *The school <u>dress code</u> prohibits short skirts.*

elementary, *adjective*: primary; basic; fundamental.

> ✦ *<u>Elementary</u> school begins with kindergarten.*

field trip, *noun*: an organized trip a class takes away from campus.

> ✦ *We took several <u>field trips</u> to local museums.*

report card, *noun*: the academic record of students.

> ✦ *Miyuki's <u>report card</u> shows that she got all As.*

role model, *noun*: a person to admire or imitate; one who sets a good example.

> ✦ *My father is a great <u>role model</u> because he works hard and spends time with his family.*

tutor, *noun*: a private teacher who helps a student outside of regular class.

> ✦ *My TOEFL <u>tutor</u> gave me extra help with my English lessons after school.*

ACTIVITY 3: ASK MORE QUESTIONS

A. Select five words from the vocabulary list and write a question for each word. Remember to start your question with a question word (Who, What, Where, When, Why, How, Is, Are, Do, Did, Does, etc.). You will also want to end each question with a question mark (?). Underline each vocabulary word.

 Example: Where is the school <u>campus</u>?

1. ....

2. ....

3. ....

4. ....

5. ....

B. Take turns asking and answering questions with your partner or group members.

ACTIVITY 4: PHOTOGRAPHS TO START CONVERSATIONS

Photographs capture moments, inform viewers, and start conversations. In small groups, examine the photograph and discuss the questions that follow.

1. Can you describe this picture?

2. Have you ever seen a yellow school bus? Where?

3. Do you prefer taking a public bus or a public train?

4. As a student, have you taken a tour bus? Where did you go?

5. Would you prefer to ride on an American yellow school bus or a British red double-decker bus? Why?

6. What do you think is the best way to get to school? Why?

ACTIVITY 5: PARAPHRASING PROVERBS

A. Read the following proverbs, and discuss them with your partner. What do they mean? Circle your favorites. Explain your choices.

1. One written word is worth a thousand pieces of gold. —Japanese

Meaning: ....

....

2. Character first, ability second. —Japanese

Meaning: ....

....

3. He who is afraid to ask is ashamed of learning. —Danish

Meaning: ....

....

4. We learn to walk by stumbling. —Bulgarian

Meaning: ....

....

5. To teach is to learn. —Japanese

Meaning: ....

....

B. Can you add another proverb related to learning and schools?

1. ....

ACTIVITY 6: PRONUNCIATION PRACTICE

You can speak English with a distinctly Japanese accent and still be clearly understood. However, reducing confusing sounds can greatly improve your communication with English speakers and help to eliminate confusion in your English conversations.

"DR" AND "DOR"

In Chapter 10 we discussed the problem of putting the "o" sound after a "d" at the end of words. This pattern should be avoided in the middle of words too. In English, when two consonants are put together, we want to make a blended sound, such as the "dr" in words like drive.

To make the "dr" sound, position your tongue so it is ready to make the "d" sound, but instead of dropping your jaw, let the air pass by your tongue as you pull it back to the "r" position.

WHICH IS RIGHT?

Try to say the following words correctly (with the "dr" pronunciation) three times and incorrectly (with the "dor" pronunciation) once. Try to mix up when you say the word incorrectly. Your partner will mark an X when they hear the incorrect version. Then switch roles.

"dr" word	1	2	3	4
drive				
drip				
drain				
drag				
drill				
drumbeat				
dry				
drop				
drown				
drew				

ACTIVITY 7: THE CONVERSATION CONTINUES

Let's continue to explore learning in school with one or two classmates. Use complete sentences to respond.

1. Did you ever have a tutor, join a study group, or go to a cram school? Why?

2. What is your earliest memory from elementary school?

3. Do you remember taking field trips? Where did you go?

4. Which school trip was your favorite? Why?

5. Do you remember any bullying at school? Do you think bullying is a problem? Why?

6. Were you often given homework? Was it too much, too little, or just right?

7. What do you usually bring to school? Why?

8. What after-school activities, clubs, or sports did you participate in?

9. What are you proud of doing in your academic studies?

10. What did you enjoy most about school? What is your favorite memory from your high school days?

11. Did you find a role model or mentor (teacher, coach) at your school? Who? Why did you choose this person?

12. Have you kept in touch with anyone from your high school? Who? How?

13. Would you want your children to attend the same schools you attended? Why or why not?

14. What makes a good school? Why? What makes a great school? Why?

15. Do you have ideas on how to change or improve schools in Japan?

ACTIVITY 8: DISCUSSING QUOTATIONS

Take turns reading these quotations out loud and discuss them with your partner. Do you agree with the quotation? Disagree? Why? Afterwards, pick a favorite quotation by circling the number and explain your choice. Remember to give a reason or example.

1. "Education is an ornament in prosperity and a refuge in adversity."
   —*Aristotle (384–322 B.C.E.), Greek philosopher*
   ☐ Agree   ☐ Disagree
   Why? ....

2. "Only the educated are free."

   —*Epictetus (55–135), Greek philosopher*

   ☐ Agree   ☐ Disagree

   Why? ....

3. "The most important thing we learn at school is the fact that the most important things can't be learned at school."

   —*Haruki Murakami (1949–), Japanese author*

   ☐ Agree   ☐ Disagree

   Why? ....

4. "Education in Japan is not intended to create people accomplished in the arts and science, but rather to manufacture the persons required by the the state."

   —*Mori Arinori (1847–1889), Japanese statesman and Japan's first education minister*

   ☐ Agree   ☐ Disagree

   Why? ....

5. "The beautiful thing about learning is that no one can take it away from you."

   —*B.B. King (1928–2015), American blues guitarist*

   ☐ Agree   ☐ Disagree

   Why? ....

6. "The highest result of education is tolerance."

   —*Helen Keller (1880–1968), American author and activist*

   ☐ Agree   ☐ Disagree

   Why? ....

7. "[In school] I encountered authority of a different kind than I had ever encountered before, and I did not like it. And they really almost got me. They came close to really beating any curiosity out of me."

   —*Steve Jobs (1955–2011), American entrepreneur and co-founder of Apple*

   ☐ Agree   ☐ Disagree

   Why? ....

8. "A child miseducated is a child lost."

   —*John F. Kennedy (1917–1963), 35th U.S. President*

   ☐ Agree   ☐ Disagree

   Why? ....

9. "I'm passionate about learning. I'm passionate about life."
   —*Tom Cruise (1962–), American actor and producer*
   ☐ Agree   ☐ Disagree
   Why? ....

10. "When love is deep, much can be accomplished."
   —*Shinichi Suzuki (1898–1998), Japanese violinist and world famous music educator*
   ☐ Agree   ☐ Disagree
   Why? ....

My favorite quote was: ....
....
Why? ....

ACTIVITY 9: TELL ME ABOUT JAPAN ... IN ENGLISH

People want to know about Japan and Japanese culture. Next time you travel abroad or meet a foreigner, you can tell them about a Japanese tradition in English.

Jukus are very well known in Japan, but many people from other countries do not have similar institutions or cram schools. How would you explain what a *juku* is to a person visiting Japan? What do you know about *jukus*? For example:

Some students only go to the *juku* to improve in problem areas, and others go for all subjects.

Think of three more things visitors to Japan might want to know about *jukus*. How can you explain these ideas?

1. ....
2. ....
3. ....

With your partner, can you ask and answer three questions about *jukus*?

For example: What subjects do they teach in a *juku*?

1Q. ....
A. ....

2Q. ....
A. ....

3Q. ....
A. ....

GRAMMAR REVIEW: CAN, MIGHT, SHOULD, MUST

Finish the sentences below in a way that reflects your opinion.

A good school can ....

A good school might ....

A good school should ....

A good school must ....

A good teacher can ....

A good teacher might ....

A good teacher should ....

A good teacher must ....

SEARCH and SHARE

Collecting Academic Advice on the Internet

Student Name: .... Date: ....

Class: .... Teacher: ....

Find a video online that provides tips for success in school or college. The video might suggest ways to improve test scores, get better grades, choose a college, get along with a roommate, or some other aspect of succeeding in school. Watch the video, take notes, and review the video for your classmates.

Video title: ....

Web address: ....

Length: .... Creator: ....

1. Describe the video.

2. What tips did the video provide?

3. Where do you think the video was produced? Why?

4. How practical did you find the advice? Why?

5. What was the strongest part? Why?

6. What was the weakest part? Why?

7. Who do you think is the best audience for this video?

8. Why did you choose this video?

9. On a scale of 1–5, with 5 being the highest, how do you rate this video? Why?

> **"Education is learning what you didn't even know you didn't know."**
> —*Daniel J. Boorstin (1914–2004), American historian*

12

EXPLORING CITIES

VOCABULARY WARM-UP

Which words do you already know? Underline them, and circle the words you are unsure about. Then review your answers with a partner.

archaeology   capital   commute   hometown   landmark
renovate   skyscraper   slum   tourist attraction   zoning

ACTIVITY 1: SHARING EXPERIENCES

Cities can be confusing, exciting, and fast paced. Some people love living in cities; some people prefer living in the countryside. Share your experiences and feelings about cities with your partner.

1. Do you still live in your hometown? Can you describe it?

2. What do you like to do in cities? What makes them fun?

3. Which big Japanese cities have you visited?

4. How can people find tourist information about Japanese cities? What do you recommend for Japanese tourists? For international tourists?

5. How do people usually get around in Japanese cities? What are some advantages of public transportation? Disadvantages?

6. What's the most northern city you have visited in Japan? Can you tell me a bit about the place?

7. What makes the capital of Japan an attractive city? Do you have a favorite area?

8. What adjectives describe Tokyo? Why did you choose them?

9. Where do you suggest international tourists visit? Why?

10. Do you recommend that tourists stay in hotels or *ryokans*? Why?

11. Why do you think so many tourists love to go to Kyoto? How has Kyoto changed over the last decade?

12. Which Japanese cities have important archaeological areas?

13. Can you compare Tokyo to Osaka? How are they similar? How are they different?

14. What about Himeji and Hiroshima? How are they similar? How are they different?

15. How is Tokyo preparing to host the 2020 Olympics? Are you excited about the 2020 Tokyo Olympics? Why?

ACTIVITY 2: EXPANDING VOCABULARY

Look at the definitions and example sentences that follow. Do the definitions match what you and your partner expected in the vocabulary warm-up list? If not, what is different?

---

archaeology, *noun*: the study of historic sites and ancient buildings.

+ *Many Japanese like to visit Egypt because of the fascinating archaeology.*

capital, *noun*: money invested and used to create more wealth.

+ *Adequate capital makes opening a new business much easier.*

capital, *noun*: a city that is the seat of government in a country or state.

+ *Tokyo is the charming capital of Japan.*

---

commute, *noun*: the time or path of travel to your job from your home and back every day.

   ✦   *My <u>commute</u> to campus is only 20 minutes by scooter.*

commute, *verb*: to travel as a commuter.

   ✦   *Sachiko uses public transportation to <u>commute</u> to work.*

hometown, *noun*: the city where a person was born.

   ✦   *Kasuga is my <u>hometown</u>, but I have lived in Fukuoka for three years.*

landmark, *noun*: a place of historical or cultural importance; a significant event or idea.

   ✦   *The Eiffel Tower in Paris, France, and the Statue of Liberty in New York City are urban <u>landmarks</u> well known around the world.*

renovate, *verb*: to make an object or place new again.

   ✦   *The government announced several projects to <u>renovate</u> the ancient site.*

skyscraper, *noun*: a high-rise building in a city; a tall office tower.

   ✦   *In 2010, Dubai built the tallest <u>skyscraper</u> in the world.*

slum, *noun*: the poor, overcrowded section of a city.

   ✦   *This fashionable neighborhood used to be a <u>slum</u>.*

tourist attraction, *noun*: an interesting sight of cultural or historical importance that brings travelers to a spot.

   ✦   *Kiyomizu-dera Temple has become one of Kyoto's greatest <u>tourist</u> <u>attractions</u>.*

zoning, *noun*: laws that restrict how property can be used in a specific area.

   ✦   *The new <u>zoning</u> laws will renovate the run-down area and reduce traffic jams on the narrow streets.*

ACTIVITY 3: ASK MORE QUESTIONS

A. Select five words from the vocabulary list and write a question for each word. Remember to start your question with a question word (Who, What, Where, When, Why, How, Is, Are, Do, Did, Does, etc.). You will also want to end each question with a question mark (?). Underline each vocabulary word.

✎ Example: What are some local <u>landmarks</u>?

1. ....

2. ....

3. ....

4. ....

5. ....

B. Take turns asking and answering questions with your partner or group members.

ACTIVITY 4: PHOTOGRAPHS TO START CONVERSATIONS

Photographs capture moments, inform viewers, and start conversations. In small groups, examine the photograph and discuss the questions that follow.

1. Can you describe this picture?

2. What does LAX stand for?

3. Have you ever seen this sign in movies? In magazines? In books?

4. Have you ever been in Los Angeles? What are some of your impressions of that city?

5. What are some airports you know?

6. Which airport is the best? Which airport is the worst? Why?

ACTIVITY 5: PARAPHRASING PROVERBS

A. Read the following proverbs, and discuss them with your partner. What do they mean? Circle your favorites. Explain your choices.

1. He who is always right will never get around the world. —Japanese

Meaning: ....

....

2. The city for wealth; the country for health. —English

Meaning: ....

....

3. Rome wasn't built in a day. —Latin

Meaning: ....

....

4. A city that sits on a hill can't be hidden. —Greek

Meaning: ....

....

5. If you are traveling toward the East, you will inevitably move away from the West. —Japanese

Meaning: ....

....

B. Can you add another proverb related to places to live?

1. ....

ACTIVITY 6: PRONUNCIATION PRACTICE

You can speak English with a distinctly Japanese accent and still be clearly understood. However, reducing confusing sounds can greatly improve your communication with English speakers and help to eliminate want to end each question with a question mark.

FINAL "I" SOUND SPELLED WITH "Y"

How can we tell the difference between the noun and verb forms? Sometimes the adjective form of a word will end with a final "i" sound—spelled with a "y". This exercise will review several words that follow this common pattern. English students often learn how to spell adjectives ending in "y" for this reason.

FINAL "K" AND FINAL "KI"

Much like the previous chapter, the difference between ending a word with a "k" sound or a "ki" sound can also be the difference between the word being a verb or a noun, or being an adjective.

When words end with a "k" sound, you do not need to make any voice. Simply pause the air in the back of your throat and let a small blast of air out quickly.

No "i" sound (noun)	"i" sound (adjective)
fun	funny
luck	lucky
yuck	yucky
smell	smelly
sun	sunny
smoke	smoky
spike	spiky
stick	sticky
pick	picky
gum	gummy

English, of course, is full of exceptions. Adding a final "i" sound to the noun "monk" gives us the very different noun "monkey." The correct adjective form of "monk" is "monkish."

No "i" sound (noun)	"i" sound (noun)
monk	monkey

Culture Corner: Names, Nicknames, and a Final "y"

Sometimes this same final "y" sound makes the difference between a male and female name, such as Jack and Jackie. However, it's more common for some males to add a final "y" in a nickname to show friendliness. For instance, some American politicians use a nickname to show a more "man of the people" image. U.S. Senator Robert F. Kennedy, the brother of U.S. President John F. Kennedy, was also known as "Bobby" Kennedy.

Almost a decade later, a little-known former southern governor asked voters and journalists to call him "Jimmy" Carter as he successfully ran for president. Likewise, the rock musician Billy Joel was born William Martin Joel, and the American actor and producer Johnny Depp was born John Christopher Depp II.

Can you think of some other celebrities who chose nicknames that end in the "y" sound for professional careers?

Jack	Jackie
Robert/ Bob	Bobby
Tom	Tommy
Bill	Billy
James/Jim	Jimmy
John	Johnny
Shigemitsu	Shiggy

Review the words below and use the correct word to complete the sentences. With your partner, find the best answer to fill in the blanks. Hint: Each sentence only uses one word.

Jack	Jackie
luck	lucky
monk	monkey
spike	spiky
stick	sticky

1. My brother has a lot of .... Last year he won the lotto!

2. Seiji is very serious and religious. When he grows up, he will probably be a Buddhist ....

3. Why is the ground so ....? Did somebody spill juice?

4. Akihiro couldn't tell if the giant spider was dead, so he decided to move it with a ....

5. My best friend growing up was a girl named ....

ACTIVITY 7: THE CONVERSATION CONTINUES

Let's continue to explore cities with one or two classmates. Use complete sentences to respond.

1. What do you expect to find in a modern city? Why?

2. Have you traveled outside of Japan? Where did you go?

3. Can you think of some famous urban landmarks? Which ones have you been to?

4. Have you ever taken a tour? When? Where did you go? What attractions did you see?

5. Do you feel safer in cities or in rural areas? Why?

6. How does archaeology help us understand cities?

7. Do you often go to museums in cities? Which ones have you visited? Which museums would you like to see and why?

8. Has any place surprised you? How was it different from what you expected?

9. Where would you like to travel next? Why?

10. Can you list five cities that have hosted the Olympic Games? Do you remember when? Do you prefer to watch the summer or the winter Olympic Games?

11. How do most people commute to work in Japan? Is it by car, by train, or by bus? Why?

12. Which city has the tallest skyscraper in Japan? Would you like to go to the top floor?

13. Are you a city person? Why?

14. What are the advantages of living in the suburbs? What are the advantages of living in cities?

15. In your opinion, what makes a city feel civilized? Why?

ACTIVITY 8: DISCUSSING QUOTATIONS

Take turns reading these quotations out loud and discuss them with your partner. Do you agree with the quotation? Disagree? Why? Afterwards, pick a favorite quotation by circling the number and explain your choice. Remember to give a reason or example.

1. "Walk around Tokyo and all you see are people trying to sell you something."
   —*Natsuo Kirino (1951–), Japanese novelist*
   ☐ Agree   ☐ Disagree
   Why? ....

2. "The people are the city."
   —*William Shakespeare (1564–1616), English playwright*
   ☐ Agree   ☐ Disagree
   Why? ....

3. "City life: millions of people being lonesome together."
   —*Henry David Thoreau (1817–1862), American writer*
   ☐ Agree   ☐ Disagree
   Why? ....

4. "I'd like to design something like a city or a museum. I want to do something hands on rather than just play golf."
   —*Brad Pitt (1963–), American actor*
   ☐ Agree   ☐ Disagree
   Why? ....

5. "Compared to U.S. cities, Japanese cities bend over backward to help foreigners. The countryside is another matter."
   —*Charles C. Mann (1955–), American journalist*
   ☐ Agree   ☐ Disagree
   Why? ....

6. "Los Angeles is a city no worse than others; a city rich and vigorous and full of pride, a city lost and beaten and full of emptiness."
   —*Raymond Chandler (1888–1959), American author*
   ☐ Agree   ☐ Disagree
   Why? ....

7. "I go to Paris, I go to London, I go to Rome, and I always say, 'There's no place like New York. It's the most exciting city in the world now.'"
   —*Robert DeNiro (1943–), American actor*
   ☐ Agree   ☐ Disagree
   Why? ....

8. "A great city is that which has the greatest men and women."
   —*Walt Whitman (1819–1892), American poet*
   ☐ Agree   ☐ Disagree
   Why? ....

9. "Until we're educating every kid in a fantastic way, until every inner city is cleaned up, there is no shortage of things to do."
   —*Bill Gates (1955–), American entrepreneur and co-founder of the Gates Foundation*
   ☐ Agree   ☐ Disagree
   Why? ....

10. "Every one of a hundred thousand cities around the world had its own special sunset and it was worth going there, just once, if only to see the sun go down."
    —*Ryu Murakami (1952–), Japanese novelist and director*
    ☐ Agree   ☐ Disagree
    Why? ....

My favorite quote was: ....

....

Why? ....

ACTIVITY 9: TELL ME ABOUT JAPAN ... IN ENGLISH

People want to know about Japan and Japanese culture. Next time you travel abroad or meet a foreigner, you can tell them about a Japanese tradition in English.

Kinkakuji is one of the most famous temples in all of Japan. What do you know about The Golden Pavilion Temple?

For example: Kinkakuji was founded in 1398 by Yoshimitsu Ashikaga.

Think of three more details visitors to Japan might want to know about Kinkakuji.

1. ....

2. ....

3. ....

With your partner, can you ask and answer three questions about the Kinkakuji?

For example: What is the best time of year to visit Kinkakuji in your opinion?

1Q. ....

A. ....

2Q. ....

A. ....

3Q. ....

A. ....

SEARCH and SHARE

Exploring a Foreign City!

Student Name: .... Date: ....

Class: .... Teacher: ....

Let's explore a foreign city together! Find an article in English about a city outside of Japan. Carefully read the article and summarize it, then bring the article to class and share some information with your classmates.

Title: ....

Author: .... Publication date: ....

Length: .... Publication: ....

1. What's the main idea?

2. How many sources were quoted?

3. Were there any illustrations? What kind?

4. What did you learn about the country where this city is located?

5. What was the most interesting part for you? Why?

6. Write down five new vocabulary words, idioms, or expressions.

    1.

    2.

    3.

    4.

    5.

7. How would you rate the article on a scale of 1–5, with 5 being the highest? Why?

8. Why did you choose this article?

"The bold adventurer succeeds the best."

—*Ovid (43 B.C.E.–17 C.E.), Roman poet*

RESOURCES & NOTES

A Note to the Conversation Teacher

How can we create more authentic, meaningful, and positive English language experiences for our conversation students?

Compelling Conversations – Japan is our fluency-focused response to that crucial question. Each activity emphasizes a different aspect of building conversations that interest and matter. The variety of short speaking tasks, pair conversations, group discussions, paraphrasing, pronunciation review, and summary activities keep students talking. The activities also encourage critical thinking and reflection while gently expanding a working vocabulary of English words. Finally, each chapter includes material specially designed for Japanese English language learners, from common pronunciation challenges to describing particular Japanese objects and traditions in English.

While we have scaffolded the short speaking and writing exercises, there is no one-size-fits-all formula for teaching English conversation skills in Japan. By alternating between personal and cultural topics and easy and difficult tasks, we hope to spark authentic communication and maintain a comfortable tempo. *Compelling Conversations – Japan* emphasizes functional fluency.

Yet each class is unique. Therefore, we also encourage you to adapt these materials to best fit your English students. Sometimes slightly modifying material can create a better rapport with your students; changing the location, verb tense, adjective, and even order of activities can make a significant difference. You are creative, dedicated educators and not mere page-turners.

Please add to, subtract from, skip, and re-order classroom activities as seems best to match the students in your English class. Each exercise can easily be modified. Conversation pair activities can become small group discussions. Pronunciation exercises and Search and Share summaries can be repeated for greater accuracy, or interviews may be extended and opinion sections reduced. The prompts here allow learners to become more autotelic—self-driven—English language learners.

Conversation classes require participation. The book's activities gently compel students to share. Everyone responds, everyone asks questions, and everyone shares experiences and research. Short summaries in the Search and Share activity can become formal videotaped presentations. (We've included some bonus reproducible presentation worksheets in the Resources section so you can easily give feedback to videotaped student presentations.) Or you may prefer to completely skip that activity to focus on other discussion activities. Be creative. Trust yourself.

Some English teachers might find 25 plus questions per chapter and five proverbs per lesson too many. Others might prefer fewer quotations or question-writing activities. We opted, however, on the side of diversity to elicit student opinions. You can reduce the choices and impose time limits. The key remains students learn by doing. We have provided a plethora of activities and alternatives. We're fond of the American expression, "It's better to have and not need than need and not have." Use or lose. The choice is up to you as you help your students gain fluency.

Encouraging, cajoling, and inspiring sometimes reluctant Japanese English language learners to speak better and clearer English—inside and outside the English classroom—can be exciting and exhausting. These speaking activities should make teaching conversation and discussion classes easier and more interesting. With your focused teaching, your students will create a lively classroom of compelling conversations. Enjoy the experience!

STUDENT PRESENTATION:
INSTRUCTOR EVALUATION

Speaker: ....

Topic: ....

Date:...................................... Time: ....

What was good to see in this presentation?

What could have been better? What still needs to be improved?

Other observations and tips:

Two tips for the student to improve their English speaking skills:

STUDENT PRESENTATION:
PEER RESPONSE AND A QUESTION

Speaker: ....

Topic: ....

Date:..   Time: ....

What was good to see in this presentation?

What could have been better? What still needs to be improved?

Other observations and tips:

Share two tips for the student presenter to do better on the next presentation.

Write a question to ask the speaker about the topic.

STUDENT PRESENTER:
SELF-EVALUATION

Speaker: ....

Topic: ....

Date:...   Time: ....

What do you think you did well in your presentation?

What could have been better? What still needs to be improved?

Other observations and tips:

What are two things you will improve in your next presentation?

CUSTOMER COMPLAINTS AND PRACTICING PREPOSITIONS

International companies often conduct business in English. Therefore, many workers need to use proper English to solve customer problems at work. In a small group, fill in the missing blank and take turns reading sentences. Is the sentence a complaint? Or is it a reply?

English prepositions can be very difficult and depend more on convention than pure logic. Therefore, the prepositions are grouped together for clarity and memorization.

To

- ✦ I'm writing .... complain about your customer service helpline.
- ✦ I'm calling .... make a complaint.
- ✦ I wish .... make an inquiry about something on my monthly bill.
- ✦ I've been trying .... get through to you for two weeks.
- ✦ The order was delivered .... the wrong branch.
- ✦ I'm sorry that I didn't get back .... you sooner.
- ✦ The delay wasn't our fault. It was due .... the bad weather.

On

- ✦ The delivery arrived .... the wrong day.
- ✦ If you can't deliver .... time, we'll have to contact other suppliers.
- ✦ I would like to apologize .... behalf of Nippon Ham for any inconvenience.

For

- ✦ Please accept our apologies .... the inconvenience.
- ✦ We would like to offer you a discount on your next order to make up .... our mistake.
- ✦ Thank you .... bringing this matter to my attention.
- ✦ I'm sorry .... sending the documents to the wrong address.
- ✦ Who signed .... the delivery?

Of

- ✦ Please find a list .... the missing items.
- ✦ There were a number .... mistakes on the invoice.
- ✦ Several .... our delivery vehicles are out of service.
- ✦ We were closed for a number .... days due to the floods.

About

- ✦ I'm sorry. I'm calling to complain .... your payment system.
- ✦ I'm calling .... my order. It isn't here yet.
- ✦ I'd like to learn .... your refund policy.

Under

+ The product is no longer .... warranty.
+ We found your order .... someone else's name.
+ Would you please look .... the counter to see if there are more?
+ I'd like to see the shirt .... the blue one.

With

+ I had some problems .... the instruction booklet.
+ .... reference to your reminder of December 1, it seems to us that an error has been made.
+ We are not satisfied .... the quality of the products.
+ I have checked .... the staff involved, and they claim they were not responsible.

In

+ .... fact, we had already paid the full bill the previous week.
+ We will do our best to make sure mistakes do not occur again .... the future.
+ Are you sure it was included .... the shipment?

Into

+ We will look .... it right away and get back to you as soon as we can.
+ I would be grateful if you could look .... the matter.

At

+ I believe your sales department is .... fault.
+ Would you please look .... the bill I received?
+ Our records show the package was received .... your address.

By

+ We strongly believe that the mistake was made .... your company.
+ We will correct the mistake .... noon today.
+ The part will be replaced .... the manufacturer.

EXERCISE B

Practice makes progress. Let's practice creating questions and sentences with prepositions tied to consumer service.

Write three questions about a consumer product with a preposition.

Example: Can you answer a question for me?

1...

2...

3...

Write three consumer complaints with a preposition and underline the preposition.

Example: How do I get a refund <u>for</u> this appliance?

1...

2...

3...

Write three responses to consumer complaints with prepositions and underline the preposition.

Example: Sorry, you will have <u>to</u> fill out this form <u>to</u> get a refund.

1...

2...

3...

RECOMMENDED ONLINE ENGLISH AS A FOREIGN LANGUAGE (EFL) RESOURCES TO KEEP LEARNING ENGLISH

Accurate English – Lisa Mojsin works on helping students improve their English through accent reduction courses. Accurate English has a particular focus on helping the troublesome areas for Japanese Learners of English.
www.accurateenglish.com

Compelling Conversations – Visit our website to keep in touch, download free ESL/EFL worksheets, and learn about more books for English Language learners.
www.CompellingConversations.com

ESL-lab – A deep, excellent resource for adult ESL students with developed listening exercises for low, intermediate, and high-intermediate students. Practical and impressive!
www.esl-lab.com

Guide to English Grammar and Writing – A valuable online collection of free tools, quizzes, and worksheets to help Capital Community college students improve their grammar and writing skills.
www.grammar.ccc.commnet.edu/grammar

Many Things – A rich resource for English language learners at multiple levels. The site includes vocabulary quizzes, proverb quizzes, and idioms games.
www.manythings.org

Online Writing Lab (OWL) – Writing tips from Purdue University's acclaimed Online Writing Lab (OWL). Includes excellent ESL tips.
www.owl.english.purdue.edu/owl

TED talks – Hear some of the world's leading experts speak about a wide variety of topics. Most talks are 15–20 minutes long, but you can start with the short talks of less than six minutes. Many videos include subtitles too.
www.Ted.com

This I Believe – This nonprofit educational website includes thousands of essays and podcasts about personal beliefs. It is widely used by American high school and college English departments to both encourage and showcase personal essays.
www.thisibelieve.com

USA Learns – This U.S. Department of Education website combines video lessons and clear written English for new English language learners worldwide.
www.usalearns.org

Voice of America – This wonderful public radio website is designed for English language learners. Short, slow radio reports look at American history, national parks, the English language, and current news.
www.voanews.com/learningenglish/home

INDEX OF QUOTATIONS

INDEX OF PROVERBS

············ ACKNOWLEDGMENTS ············

Stacey Aaronson
Toni Aberson
David Akarty
Lara Drew Akarty
Rebecca Beck
Caity Begg
Marco Blanco
Donna Brinton
Kai Aichi Craig
Gladys Cruz
Jane Dean
Dixon Apparel
Jingen Doi
Dan Dumitrache
Easy English Times
Robert Glynn
Kim Goldberg
Danny Hackin
Marshal Holmes
Hall Houston
Kaito Imai
Miyuki Imai
Yurie Ishigaki
Yukari Aoi Johnston
Richard Jones
Jo Kanda
James Keating
Yang Liu
Manami II
Daisuke Matsuoka
Lisa Mojsin
Miniami Okamoto
Eva Owen
James Polk
Steven J. Riggs
Nick Robinson
Hank Rosenfeld
Yui Shigeoka Sato
Andrea Schmidt
Laurie Selik
Kaz Shida
Sidewalk Café Venice
Gen Tateyama
Scott Tingley
Mark Treston
Jennifer Weaver-Youree
Jeff Wilson
Ben Worthington
Rie Yoshida
Ryo Yoshida
Lisa Zollner

> *It is gratefulness that makes the soul great.*
> —ABRAHAM JOSHUA HESCHEL (1907–1972)
> American rabbi and Jewish philosopher

"You have a book for Vietnam. Why don't you have one for Japan?"

This book comes from that simple question four years ago. Many friends, colleagues, and ELT professionals have helped bring this project to life. We wrote, we researched, we edited, and we field tested. Then we wrote some more and edited far more. It's been a creative collaboration among dedicated English teachers.

We've had many fine discussions and many delicious meals creating this book. Dozens of people have shared their time and thoughts. We would like to give a small hat tip to the exceptionally generous and often insightful friends and savvy professionals listed to the left.

Some English teachers offered advice, others recommended resources, and many readers gave detailed notes improving the ESL textbook. Some simply encouraged us to continue and shared positive experiences with previous versions of *Compelling Conversations*. We benefited—in tangible and invisible ways—from every email exchange and illuminating discussion. Thank you.

We hope this book meets and exceeds your expectations. If this conversation book realizes its goals of helping more Japanese English language learners become more fluent in our strange native tongue, it will be partly because of your contribution. Your insights helped, and we remain grateful.

We listened and learned to the best of our abilities and resources. We have done our best, and we feel satisfied. Mistakes and missteps, however, may remain. If so, we take full responsibility. Thank you for your time, energy, and help.

Eric H. Roth, Shiggy Ichinomiya, and Brent Warner
Co-authors
August, 2015

AUTHOR PROFILES

ERIC H. ROTH teaches international graduate students the pleasures and perils of academic writing and public speaking in English at the University of Southern California (USC). He also advises the ALI Conversation Group program and co-authors the *Compelling Conversations* textbook series. Roth has taught English and writing courses for over 20 years.

Awarded a full scholarship as a Lilly Scholar, Roth studied philosophy and American history at Wabash College (1980–1984) and received his M.A. in Media Studies from the New School (1988). A former journalist and Congressional aide in New York City, Roth has taught English to high school, community college, adult, and university students since moving to Los Angeles in 1990. Highlights of his teaching career include: teaching the first Saturday morning citizenship class in Santa Monica (1994); directing the CES Adult Education Center (1995–1998); working with international students in summer IEP programs at UCLA Extension (1997–2000, 2003–2005); teaching USC engineering students in Madrid, Spain (2007) and Paris, France (2008); directing the APU International High School in Ho Chi Minh City, Vietnam (2009); winning two USC Teaching with Technology grants (2012); and being promoted to master lecturer at USC (2013).

Roth co-authored *Compelling Conversations: Questions and Quotations on Timeless Topics* in 2006 to help English language learners increase their English fluency. Recommended by *English Teaching Professional* magazine, the advanced fluency-focused textbook has been used in over 50 countries in English classrooms and conversation clubs. *Easy English Times*, an adult literacy newspaper, has also published a conversation activities column by Roth since 2008.

After directing an elite private high school summer program in Vietnam in 2009, Roth co-authored the first country-specific version of the *Compelling Conversations* series for Vietnam in 2011. He wrote *Compelling American Conversations: Questions and Quotations for Intermediate American English Language Learners* the following year for American immigrants and international college students. An active member of California Teachers of English to Speakers of Other Languages (CATESOL) and the international professional organization Teachers of English to Speakers of Other Languages (TESOL), Roth has given many presentations at local, state, and international conferences. Roth hopes to work with other experienced English teachers and material writers to provide additional *Compelling Conversations* titles for specific countries. *Compelling Conversations – Japan* is his fourth book for Chimayo Press.

SHIGGY ICHINOMIYA is a professional photographer, recreational triathlete, and English materials writer. Born in Kobe, Japan, to a Japanese father and German mother and raised primarily in London, England, Ichinomiya graduated with an English literature degree from Boston University in 1991.

Ichinomiya moved to Japan and learned Japanese as a second language. This achievement helped him better serve students during his ten years of teaching English in Kobe, Osaka, and Nagoya. Eventually, he mastered over 1,945 kanji characters to read a newspaper and became fluent in Japanese. During his diverse English teaching career, he worked as an English language immersion teacher for the Hyogo Prefectural Government, the YMCA and YWCA, Shoei Women's College, Shinwa High School, Kawasaki Heavy Industries, and Proctor and Gamble. He also privately tutored a wide range of students, from children, teenagers, and housewives to doctors, business executives, and city officials. Realizing a personal dream, Ichinomiya also appeared regularly on the Japanese afternoon variety TV show Wide ABCDE~SU from 2000–2001.

Returning to the United States in 2001, Ichinomiya became a professional photographer/videographer. He also created the GoShiggyGo.com website in 2012. Ichinomiya has completed two Ironman triathlons (2010, 2013). A member of CATESOL and TESOL, he is the co-author of *Compelling Conversations – Japan.* He lives in Los Angeles, regularly runs, and loves his pit bull Cali-Blu. GoSpeakGo.com is his latest website creation.

BRENT WARNER has recently joined USC (his alma mater)—where he received his Masters in Teaching English as a Second or Other Language—as a full-time faculty member. His passion for ESL/EFL started when Warner took his first Japanese course in college and learned the importance of a good language teacher. Warner received a scholarship to study at Gunma University and ended up living in Japan on and off for 12 years. The majority of his time was spent teaching at the college/university or business levels. Warner began to incorporate technology into his lessons, finding that he could make the lessons more engaging and stronger for everyone involved.

This passion for blending education and technology led Warner to found www.EdTech.tv —a website that works as a teacher training tool for educators who want to implement technology into their own classes. His weekly podcast has won critical acclaim and a niche audience of serious educators. Warner also worked as the Academic Manager of Kaplan International, where he contributed to the center's status as the #1 ranked Kaplan International worldwide. His responsibilities included supervising English teachers and monitoring college preparation courses. He currently volunteers for CATESOL Orange County often leads CATESOL workshops. Warner is the author of the EFL ebook, *How to Pass the TOEFLibt Test* (2012) and co-author of *Compelling Conversations – Japan.*

EDITORS

After 35 years of teaching English and supervising English teachers, TONI ABERSON (M.A. English; M.A. Psychology and Religion) believes that a lively classroom is the optimal learning environment. "If people are thinking, sharing, and laughing, then they're learning," notes Aberson. "The mere fact that those adults are in an English classroom attests to their courage and their determination to learn. Adult English students bring a wealth of interesting experiences with them," continues Aberson. "They bring the world into the classroom. The challenge for English teachers is to put students at ease and encourage them to practice English. What better way than to ask students about their lives? I love teaching English."

After retiring and moving close to the beach, Aberson has started a second career as an ESL/EFL author and editor. She is the co-author of *Compelling Conversations: Questions and Quotations on Timeless Topics* (2006), *Compelling American Conversations: Questions and Quotations for Intermediate American English Language Learners* (2012), and *It's A Breeze: 42 Lively English Lessons on American Idioms* (2012).

LAURIE A. SELIK is a nonprofit professional with experience providing strategic leadership, creating fundraising plans, writing award-winning grants, and developing authentic relationships with donors. She is currently manager of foundation and corporate giving at The Colburn School in Los Angeles, where she implements and directs the school's institutional giving strategies. Selik worked for ten years in public radio, reinvigorating foundation support for American Public Media's *Marketplace*, public radio's business program, and launched *Weekend America*, where she was managing producer. Selik continues to consult in public radio and manages foundation support for *Localore* produced by AIRmedia, and often lends her nonprofit management skills to nonprofit boards.

Selik is also the co-publisher at Chimayo Press. She holds a master of professional writing degree from the University of Southern California and a bachelor of arts degree in communications from Michigan State University. Selik is currently writing *Compelling Conversations for Fundraisers: Talk Your Way to Success with Donors and Funders* (2016).

CONTRIBUTOR

RICHARD JONES is the founder of TextEdit USA, which provides editing and proofreading services for international scholars publishing in English. He also teaches academic writing courses at Cal State Fullerton and the University of Southern California. Richard lived in Japan from 1998–2008 where he worked as an editor and English teacher. He has an M.Ed. in TESOL (Teaching English to Speakers of Other Languages) from Temple University, Japan, and an M.A. in East Asian Studies with a concentration on Japanese Literature and Culture from UCLA. Richard has also played music with bands in both the U.S. and Japan and spends his free time cooking, writing, and tending to his cats.

"In my own teaching, I have found questions and quotations to be highly effective in promoting student discussion. Questions are useful in that they require a response from the listener. Asking them also helps students master the tricky rules of the interrogative. Quotations are brilliant flashes of wit expressed in the shortest space possible, often just a sentence or two. The authors have compiled a formidable collection of quotations by famous people. The authors also add some wise proverbs here and there. My two favourites were 'Recite *patience* three times and it will spare you a murder' and 'When money talks, truth keeps silent,' which are from Korea and Russia. In sum, *Compelling Conversations* is a recommended resource for teachers who want to make their conversation classes more learner-centered. It should be especially appealing to those who wish to escape the confines of the Presentation-Practice-Production approach and do without a formal grammatical or functional syllabus. It reflects the authors' considerable professional experience, and would be a notable addition to any English teacher's bookshelf."

—Hall Houston
English Teaching Professional magazine (January 2009)

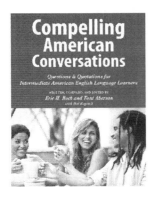

"How can so much learning be in just one book? *Compelling American Conversations* is all that an ESL teacher or student needs to use in their course. With clear, easy-to-follow directions, students learn necessary details about American English and culture, practice critical thinking, and expand vocabulary and idioms as they converse in real, natural adult English. Included in the "Search and Share" component are marvelous lessons on using the Internet. An extra bonus is that any of the conversations, quotes, etc. can be used as writing prompts. The book is fun and stimulating and, fortunately, very accessible for the intermediate learner."

—Planaria Price
Author, *Life in the USA* and *Realistically Speaking*

"Often it is the duty of the ESL speaking and listening teacher to tailor the text to their class culture and demographics; therefore, it is a novel idea to produce a textbook for speaking skills of a particular English language learner ... Roth and Aberson have employed such an approach for Vietnamese ELLs in *Compelling Conversations: Questions and Quotations for Advanced Vietnamese English Language Learners* ... [It] is a text that encourages multiculturalism, is flexible enough to use for all ages of advanced English learners, and gives a personally relevant, tailored experience for students to formulate their opinions in anticipation of present and future communications with English speakers ..."

—Sarah Elizabeth Snyder, Northern Arizona University
Teaching English as a Second Language – Electronic Journal, September 2012

ABOUT CHIMAYO PRESS

Sophisticated English for Global Souls

CHIMAYO PRESS is an independent educational publishing company committed to publishing niche books that create compelling conversations, deepen relationships, and celebrate the human spirit. We launched in 2005 with one advanced level English as a Second Language (ESL) title—*Compelling Conversations: Questions and Quotations on Timeless Topics*—from authors Eric H. Roth and Toni Aberson. This fluency-focused textbook has blossomed into a series that meets the varying needs of English language learners and their teachers in over 50 countries. It has also become the foundation for an expanding number of ESL and EFL (English as a Foreign Language) titles.

As a small publisher, we are grateful for each purchase of our books. We have a growing list of both nonfiction and fiction titles—our authors include working English teachers, radio professionals, and screenwriters, and each book reflects the passion and perspectives of the authors. Visit www.ChimayoPress.com to see our growing catalog. English language teachers, tutors, and students are also invited to visit www.compellingconversations.com for more conversation materials, audio downloads, and teacher tips.

Chimayo Press is named for our amazingly communicative, talented, and loving first border collie. We met Chimayo soon after a visit to the inspirational New Mexico town on a cross-country trip from Chicago to Los Angeles. That's Chimayo's image in our logo.

Would you like to review this book? We'd love to receive your feedback and start another new conversation!

Made in the USA
Lexington, KY
28 November 2016